Modern Budgeting

ORGANISATION FOR ECONOMIC CO-OPERATION AND DEVELOPMENT

ORGANISATION FOR ECONOMIC CO-OPERATION AND DEVELOPMENT

Pursuant to Article 1 of the Convention signed in Paris on 14th December 1960, and which came into force on 30th September 1961, the Organisation for Economic Co-operation and Development (OECD) shall promote policies designed:

- to achieve the highest sustainable economic growth and employment and a rising standard of living in Member countries, while maintaining financial stability, and thus to contribute to the development of the world economy;
- to contribute to sound economic expansion in Member as well as non-member countries in the process of economic development; and
- to contribute to the expansion of world trade on a multilateral, non-discriminatory basis in accordance with international obligations.

The original Member countries of the OECD are Austria, Belgium, Canada, Denmark, France, Germany, Greece, Iceland, Ireland, Italy, Luxembourg, the Netherlands, Norway, Portugal, Spain, Sweden, Switzerland, Turkey, the United Kingdom and the United States. The following countries became Members subsequently through accession at the dates indicated hereafter: Japan (28th April 1964), Finland (28th January 1969), Australia (7th June 1971), New Zealand (29th May 1973), Mexico (18th May 1994), the Czech Republic (21st December 1995), Hungary (7th May 1996), Poland (22nd November 1996) and the Republic of Korea (12th December 1996). The Commission of the European Communities takes part in the work of the OECD (Article 13 of the OECD Convention).

Publié en français sous le titre :
BUDGÉTISATION MODERNE

FOREWORD

This report provides an interpretation by Dr. Allen Schick of the Brookings Institution, Washington, D.C., of recent budgeting reforms in five Member countries: Australia, France, New Zealand, Sweden and the United Kingdom.

The main work for this report was conducted in 1994 and 1995; hence the report may not take sufficient account of more recent developments. Efforts have been made to incorporate developments that occurred after the work was completed. These include Prime Minister Juppe's initiatives in France and the report of the National Commission of Audit in Australia.

The report was prepared by Jon Blondal of the OECD Public Management Service. Technical assistance was provided by Jocelyne Feuillet-Allard and Judy Zinnemann.

The views expressed are those of the author and do not commit or necessarily reflect those of governments of OECD Member countries. This report is published on the responsibility of the Secretary-General of the OECD.

TABLE OF CONTENTS

EXECUTIVE SUMMARY

The management revolution that is restructuring the public sector in the OECD community has been under way for more than a decade in some countries and is only starting in others. The duration of this revolution attests to the difficulty of uprooting old rules and habits, as well as to the staying power and determination of reformers. The task has not been completed in any of the countries that have sought to transform public administration, but in none is there serious risk of abandoning reform and reverting to the traditional command and control relationship between the centre of government and public agencies and between the centre of departments and operating units.

In the five countries examined in this report – Australia, France, New Zealand, Sweden and the United Kingdom – there is professed consensus within government that the centralised model no longer suits the needs and conditions of public management. Reform has been centred around accountability frameworks in which the government entrusts spending agencies with flexibility in using resources, in exchange for holding them responsible for results. The repertoire of devices for enforcing managerial accountability includes strategic and operational plans, performance measures and targets, contracts for personal and organisational performance, de-coupling service delivery from policy making, new accounting rules and annual reports, more active use of evaluation and auditing, and financial inducements and sanctions.

The five countries have different governing traditions and have approached reform differently. France has a long tradition of detailed supervision by financial controllers, and it has moved cautiously to enlarge the operational discretion of local managers. There is substantial evidence of progress as the reforms move from the experimental stage to implementation across the public sector. Sweden is at the other end of the spectrum, for it has a long history of small ministries and relatively autonomous agencies. Sweden gives managers more latitude than is found in some other countries, so that, although the innovations have been less dramatic than elsewhere, they have been effective. On the eve of reform, more than a dozen years ago, the United Kingdom had already retreated from the doctrine of Treasury Control that it had practised for more than a century. Its financial management initiative launched in 1982, the Next Steps initiative commenced half a dozen years later, and the fundamental expenditure reviews now under way have been spurred by political support at the top of the government for re-shaping the public sector. Australia entered the reform era with highly centralised controls, but in the past dozen years it has discarded many personnel and financial restrictions and adopted a variety of political and administrative arrangements to stimulate management improvement. As a small country with an open economy, New Zealand felt its future well-being threatened by powerful international forces, and it responded by creatively adapting commercial practices to public management.

The five countries face similar problems in restructuring national administration. All must establish new relationships between the centre, which is politically accountable for governmental performance, and operating units, where services are provided and most resources are spent. Defining this new relationship has been difficult because strategic controls must be devised in place of the discredited *ex ante* controls. In visits to the five countries, the view was sometimes put that once central intervention in administrative details has ended, spending agencies should be free to chart their own course without substantial direction from the top. This is a naive and wrong-minded view which, if not challenged, may undermine or discredit reform. The point must be made that reform does not open the door to an "anything goes" attitude to public money. But the fact that complaints about central interference persist in the face of a truly massive withdrawal of central organs from the details of expenditure highlights the difficulty of defining new roles and relationships. Most countries have had difficulty drawing a clear line between the responsibilities of central and operating institutions.

Each country faces considerable pressure on its operating budget. In fact, running costs (adjusted for inflation) and staffing levels have declined over the past decade. The trend has given spending agencies mixed messages. On the one hand, it has spurred them to actively search for efficiencies; but on the other, it has generated some apprehension that the reforms have more to do with cutting resources than with improving management. This concern emerges in conflicts over efficiency dividends (Australia), cash limits (the United Kingdom), and mandated spending cuts (Sweden).

All of the countries must motivate managers to take initiative and responsibility over what they spend and produce and to accept that the performance of their organisation depends on their personal performance. There has been an enormous turnover of senior and middle managers in New Zealand and the United Kingdom, as many officials discomfited by the new managerialism have left on their own accord or have been encouraged to depart. The importation of new managers appear to be inconsequential in France and Australia. Each government must determine what is acceptable risk, as operating agencies are given discretion to spend resources and take other actions that may have important political of financial ramifications. This issue is least troublesome in Sweden, where the line between ministries and agencies is well marked, and most pressing in New Zealand and the United Kingdom, where the independence of agencies has called into question the Westminster doctrine of ministerial accountability.

In all of the countries, restructuring is seen as a long-term effort to change managerial behaviour and organisational culture. The initial steps, entailing procedural changes, such as the divestiture of *ex ante* controls, have been relatively easy. With the exception of France, this stage has been largely completed. France is lagging because it started later than the others and it must overcome the strong tradition of running the country from the centre. The second part of the bargain – getting civil servants to manage for results and transforming state agencies into performance-driven producers of public services – is taking much more time. One may wonder whether, in the absence of market discipline, this objective will ever be fully attained. Even when a management ethic has taken hold, as it has in several of the countries reviewed here, one cannot be sure that it has been institutionalised.

Each government has devised an instrument of choice to assure that performance information influences organisational behaviour. Australia relies on a heavy dose of programme evaluation both before policies have been initiated and after they have been funded; France is emphasising responsibility centres as a means of imbuing civil servants with awareness that their actions can make a difference in the quality of service; Sweden has placed increasing reliance on annual reports that are audited for reliability of financial and performance statements; the United Kingdom looks to framework documents and performance targets to concentrate managerial attention on key objectives and results; New Zealand invests considerable resources in negotiating performance agreements for chief executives and purchase agreements for agencies. Every country faces the problem that no matter how much it generates by way of performance information, decisions may be taken and resources allocated in disregard of objectives and results.

The introduction of new methods has also aimed at invigorating the reform effort. To restructure management the government must demonstrate its continuing commitment to the task and sustain interest among senior and middle managers. Precisely because implanting a performance ethic takes more than a decade, it does not suffice for the government to announce an initiative and then let matters run their course. At frequent intervals the last steps must be renewed by new steps.

Because of the difficulty of implanting a performance culture, every country has had a spate of disappointments; none has accomplished everything it set out to do. The United Kingdom learned that FMI had produced better information, but had done little to liberate managers at operating levels; it subsequently learned that Next Steps had energised the newly established agencies but had not yet transformed the central departments. Australia has been vexed by the problem of packaging performance information into a useful format, and it has also been disappointed by the less than optimal use of the programme structure. New Zealand has made relatively little headway in measuring outcomes, and the relationship between ministers purchasing services and agencies supplying them has not been sufficiently clarified. Sweden has been disappointed by the failure of the multi-year budget frames to deepen the quality of budget work. France has found that, despite government guidelines, some important ministries have dragged their feet in devolving responsibility to local agencies. In each country there is ample scope for complaint and criticism, but the disappointments should not blind us to the enormous progress that has been made. Because the reforms have been so ambitious, they are bound to fall somewhat short of the mark.

One of the most encouraging characteristics of the reforms is that they have not been treated by public managers as just the latest in a long series of managerial fads. They welcome the reforms and relate them to the quality of their work and the satisfaction they get from the job. Support for reform has persisted at ministerial level and in senior official ranks. It would be unrealistic to expect ministers to regard management innovation as uppermost on their political agenda, but they accord it high priority in several of the countries and demonstrate interest in all.

Beyond the impressionistic evidence, there is strong reason to believe that restructuring public management has brought sizeable efficiency gains that are reflected in lower staffing levels and reductions in real operating expenditures. Many agencies are doing more with less. While hidden reductions in service levels or quality have certainly occurred, few agencies have compensated for lost resources by cutting services. The growing practice of publishing output plans and results discourages agencies from lowering service standards when faced with resource constraints, but an even more important influence has been the spread of managerial responsibility in service agencies. It is hard to form a judgement on how the managerial changes have affected programme outcomes. While there is no reason to suspect that outcomes have been adversely affected by the reforms, neither is there a basis for claiming that they have been improved.

OVERVIEW

The management revolution that is restructuring the public sector in many OECD Member countries has been under way for more than a decade in some countries and is only starting in others. The duration of this revolution attests to the difficulty of uprooting old rules and habits, as well as to the staying power and determination of reformers. The task has not been completed in any of the countries that have sought to transform public administration, but in none is there serious risk of abandoning reform and reverting to the traditional command-and-control relationship between the centre of government and public agencies and between the centre of departments and operating units. The traditional governing structure concentrated control of human and financial resources at the centre and operational responsibility for delivering services at the bottom of organisations. At one end of government were the controllers, at the other end the controlled. The centre issued rules, monitored compliance with the rules, and intervened as it thought appropriate; the operating echelons complied, or at least pretended to. With control in one place and responsibility for producing in another, public sector managers often were managers in name only. Some of the more venturesome became skilled in outwitting the controllers, others merely complied. Many undoubtedly sought to do as much public good as they could within the constraints they faced.

This arrangement governed not only the management of expenditure but other administrative operations as well, especially those pertaining to the recruitment and remuneration of staff. As outmoded as it may appear to some today, command-and-control public administration grew out of two widely shared values: a determination by governments to restrain the growth in public employment and expenditure and a commitment to assure uniformity and consistency in the provision of public services. Whatever these virtues, the first objective has been overtaken by the vast expansion in the scope of government, particularly in transfers and grants; the second has been largely accomplished. With the growth of government, the centre became increasingly cluttered by detail, diverting policy and managerial attention from larger programme and financial matters.

Many national governments eased central control in the decades after World War II by consolidating items of expenditure into broader categories and giving agencies somewhat greater flexibility in using resources. Some attempted to strengthen budgeting as a policy process through innovations such as planning-programming-budgeting (PPB) systems, but these top-down reforms generally were unsuccessful and they did little or nothing to improve managerial capacity at operating levels. The current spate of reforms, by contrast, does aim to improve public sector management. They are centred around accountability frameworks in which the government entrusts spending agencies with flexibility in using resources, in exchange for holding them responsible for results. The repertoire of devices for enforcing managerial accountability includes strategic and operational plans, performance measures and targets, contracts for personal and organisational performance, decoupling service delivery from policymaking, new accounting rules and annual reports, more active use of evaluation and auditing, and financial inducements and sanctions. The mix of new instruments varies among the countries that have ventured along these lines, but in all there has been marked devolution of financial and overall managerial control and the introduction of novel arrangements for holding agencies and managers to account.

In the five countries examined in this report – Australia, France, New Zealand, Sweden and the United Kingdom – there is professed consensus within government that the centralised model no longer suits the needs and conditions of public management. What is needed is less rigidity in the provision of services and more responsiveness to local conditions and customer preferences. Rigid rules, it is widely agreed, have impeded adoption of the best available practices and have forced managers to settle instead for middling uniformity. It is important to acknowledge, however, that traditional public administration still is favoured in some prominent OECD Member countries where centralised financial and personnel control is regarded as a virtue. Germany and Japan may fit this model, as do some smaller Member countries.

Although the sample discussed in this report is small, the five countries span three of the main political-administrative cultures found in the OECD community: the Westminster system, the French administrative tradition and the Scandinavian model. The American separation-of-powers form of government is not included because its administrative "reinvention" was in its early stages when the research was conducted in 1994 and 1995. The German bureaucratic model is excluded because that country has taken few steps to decentralise management in the Federal Republic, perhaps because its attention to the complex task of unification has crowded out some other governmental matters.

Not only do the five countries reviewed here have different governing traditions, they also had different administrative arrangements before restructuring commenced. France has a long tradition of detailed supervision by financial controllers stationed in the Ministry of Finance, and it has moved cautiously to enlarge the operational discretion of local managers. It lags behind the other countries because it started somewhat later and has had much further to go. But there is substantial evidence of progress as the reforms move from the experimental stage to implementation across the public sector. Sweden is at the other end of the spectrum, for it has a long history of small ministries and relatively autonomous agencies. Sweden gives managers more latitude than is found in some other countries, so that although the innovations have been less dramatic than elsewhere, they have been effective. The three Commonwealth countries are sufficiently differentiated in administrative practices and in their reforms to justify a separate look each. At the eve of reform, more than a dozen years ago, the United Kingdom had already retreated from the doctrine of Treasury Control that it had practised for more than a century. Its Financial Management Initiative launched in 1982, the Next Steps initiative commenced half a dozen years later and the recent Fundamental Expenditure Reviews have all been spurred by political support at the top of the government for reshaping the public sector. Australia entered the reform era with highly centralised controls, but in the past dozen years it has discarded many personnel and financial restrictions and adopted a variety of political and administrative arrangements to stimulate management improvement. As a small country with an open economy, New Zealand felt its future well-being threatened by powerful international forces, and it responded by creatively adapting commercial practices to public management.

THE TASK OF REFORM

The five countries have faced similar problems in restructuring their national administration. All must redefine relationships between the centre, which is politically accountable for governmental performance, and operating units where services are provided and most resources are spent. Defining this new relationship has been difficult because new management procedures must be devised in place of the discredited *ex ante* controls. The new controls must safeguard the government's interest in total expenditure and programme priorities, and they must also promote efficiency in public management and quality in service delivery. In visits to the five countries, this writer sometimes encountered the view that once central intervention in administrative details has ended, spending agencies should be free to chart their own course without substantial direction from the top. This is a naive and wrong-minded view which, if not challenged, may undermine or discredit reform. The point must be made that reform does not open the door to an "anything goes" attitude to public money. But the fact that complaints about central interference persist in the face of a truly massive withdrawal of central organs from the details of expenditure highlights the difficulty of defining new roles and relationships. With the exception of Sweden, which has long-standing and established division of labour between ministries and agencies, every country has had difficulty drawing a clear line between the responsibilities of central and operating institutions.

Each country faces considerable pressure on its operating budget. In fact, running costs (adjusted for inflation) and staffing levels have declined over the past decade. The trend has given spending agencies mixed messages. On the one hand, it has spurred them to actively search for efficiencies; but on the other, it has generated some apprehension that the reforms have more to do with cutting resources than with improving management. The concern emerges in conflicts over efficiency dividends (Australia), cash limits (United Kingdom), mandated spending cuts (Sweden) and the adequacy of spending levels (New Zealand).

All of the countries must motivate managers to take initiative and responsibility for what they spend and produce and to accept that the performance of their organisation depends on their personal performance. There has been an enormous turnover of senior and middle managers in New Zealand and the United Kingdom, as many officials discomfited by the new managerialism have left on their own accord or have been encouraged to depart. Many of the new managers have had substantial work experience in the private sector and are more at home in the new regime than they would have been in the old administrative structures. The importation of new managers appears to be inconsequential in France and Australia. These two countries, along with Sweden, seem to have confidence that "letting managers manage" suffices; the United Kingdom and New Zealand have acted on the presumption that it is necessary to "make managers manage". Each government must determine what is acceptable risk, as operating agencies are given discretion to spend resources and take other actions that may have important political or financial ramifications. This issue is least troublesome in Sweden, where the line between ministries and agencies is well marked, and most pressing in the United Kingdom, where the new independence of agencies has called into question the Westminster doctrine of ministerial accountability.

In all of the countries, restructuring is seen as a long-term effort to change managerial behaviour and organisational culture. The initial steps, entailing procedural changes such as the divestiture of *ex ante* controls, were relatively easy. With the exception of France, this stage has been largely completed. France is lagging because it started later than the others and it must overcome the strong tradition of running the country from the centre. The second part of the bargain – getting civil servants to manage for results and transforming state agencies into performance-driven producers of public services – has taken much more time. One may wonder whether, in the absence of market discipline, this objective will ever be fully attained. Even when a management ethic has taken hold, as it has in several of the countries reviewed here, one cannot be sure that it has been institutionalised. A change in leadership or in the circumstances facing an agency, a budget crisis or other factors may swiftly undo years of progress. Perhaps it will only be when the reform era has closed and the innovations have become routines of public management that the commitment to performance will be truly tested.

Each government has devised an instrument of choice to ensure that performance information influences organisational behaviour. Australia relies on a heavy dose of programme evaluation, both before policies have been initiated and after they have been funded. France is emphasising responsibility centres as a means of imbuing civil servants with awareness that their actions can make a difference in the quality of service; Sweden has placed increasing reliance on annual reports that are audited for reliability of financial and performance statements; the United Kingdom looks to framework documents and performance targets to concentrate managerial attention on key objectives and results; New Zealand invests considerable resources in negotiating performance agreements for chief executives and purchase agreements for agencies. In the four countries that have had extended experience, today's favoured instrument was not yesterday's. There is much evidence of trial and error and of willingness to try out new approac hes in the hope that they will prove more effective than previous ones. The search for new methods arises out of a fundamental gap between producing performance information and acting on the basis of performance. Every country faces the problem that no matter how much it generates by way of performance information, decisions may be taken and resources allocated in disregard of objectives and results. Australia is trying to narrow this gap by closely linking programme evaluation to policy work in the Cabinet; Sweden has enhanced the role of auditors (who are responsible to the Ministry of Finance) in examining agency performance; the United Kingdom has placed increasing weight on the selection of both Next Steps and Citizens Charter targets and on comparing results to targets. New Zealand reviews departmental Key Result Areas (KRAs) in the light of government-wide Strategic Result Areas (SRAs).

The introduction of new methods has also aimed at invigorating the reform effort. To restructure management, the government must demonstrate its continuing commitment to the task and sustain interest among senior and middle managers. Precisely because implanting a performance ethic takes more than a decade, it does not suffice for the government to announce an initiative and then let matters run their course. At frequent intervals – the experience thus far suggests no more than four to five years apart – the last steps must be renewed by new steps. If business management is a guide, performance-driven agencies may be in a continuing state of flux with only a few years between one wave of reforms and the next.

New Zealand also fits this pattern, even though it legislated a full menu of changes at the start. The reforms enacted in 1988 and 1989 were comprehensive in scope, but they were established in law, not merely in government guidance or exhortation. Nevertheless, New Zealand also has fine-tuned its reforms in the light of experience. In fact, most of the procedures now used by New Zealand departments were initiated after the legislated reforms had been enacted.

Because of the difficulty of implanting a performance culture, every country has had a spate of disappointments; none has accomplished everything it set out to do. The United Kingdom learned that the financial Management Initiative (FMI) had produced better information, but had done little to liberate managers at operating levels; it subsequently learned that Next Steps had energised the newly established agencies but had not yet transformed the central departments. Australia has been vexed by the problem of packaging performance information into a useful format, and it has also been disappointed by the apparent useless-ness of the programme structure; New Zealand has made relatively little headway in measuring outcomes, and the relationship between ministers purchasing ser-vices and agencies supplying them has not been sufficiently clarified. Sweden has been disappointed by the failure of the multi-year budget frames to deepen the quality of budget work; France has found that despite government guidelines, some important ministries have dragged their feet in devolving responsibility to local agencies. In each country there is ample scope for complaint and criticism, but the disappointments do not hide the fact that enormous progress has been made. Because the reforms have been so ambitious, they are bound to fall somewhat short of the mark.

To this observer one of the most encouraging characteristics of the reforms is that they have not been treated by public managers as just the latest in a long series of managerial fads. They have welcomed the reforms and have related them to the quality of their work and the satisfaction they get from the job. Support for reform has persisted at ministerial level and in senior official ranks. It would be unrealistic to expect ministers to regard management innovation as uppermost on their political agenda, but they have accorded it moderately high priority in several of the countries and have demonstrated interest in all.

Beyond the impressionistic evidence, there is strong reason to believe that restructuring public management has brought sizeable efficiency gains that are reflected in lower staffing levels and reductions in real operating expenditures. Many agencies are doing more with less. While hidden reductions in service levels or quality have certainly occurred, few agencies have compensated for lost resources by cutting services. The growing practice of publishing performance targets and results discourages agencies from degrading services in the face of resource constraints, but an even more important influence has been the spread of managerial responsibility in service agencies. It is hard to form a judgement on how the managerial changes have affected programme outcomes. While there is no reason to suspect that outcomes have been adversely affected by the reform, neither is there a strong basis for claiming that they have been improved.

MARKETS AND MANAGERS

The five countries have taken two broad approaches to improving public sector performance. One has been to apply or stimulate market behaviour in government agencies; the other has been to empower and motivate managers to improve performance. The market-type mechanisms include privatisation and contracting out, accrual accounting and cost recovery, and contracts for individual or group performance. The array of management tools include planning and evaluation, devolution and flexibility in using resources, targeting and measuring performance, and corporate planning and programme evaluation. Every country has its feet in both camps, but the mix of approaches varies. New Zealand has embraced market principles more rigorously than any other country, and it has sought to stimulate market discipline by distinguishing between the government as owner and the government as purchaser, by levying a capital charge for the government's financial investment, by contracting for the services of chief executives, and by negotiating purchase agreements for the "sale" of output from agencies to ministries. France hews most closely to a managerial model, empowering responsibility centres to operate as quasi-autonomous units. Government in the United Kingdom has espoused a market ethic, but it also places great reliance on managers accepting responsibility for their work and performance. Australia and Sweden tilt to the management end of the spectrum, yet both have given scope to user charges, commercialisation and other market-type mechanisms.

The differences between the two approaches should not be overstated, for, after all, governments do not operate in genuine markets. Yet the two approaches pull in different directions. A managerial posture puts great confidence in "letting managers manage"; a market approach insists on "making managers manage". The first relies on empowering managers to take initiative and responsibility; the second relies on prices and contracts to compel efficiency and accountability. The extent to which market-type behaviour can be induced in the public sector is being tested by the New Zealand reforms. Simulated markets are not real markets, and contracts between government entities (such as framework documents in the United Kingdom and purchase agreements in New Zealand) are not the same as truly arms-length agreements between unrelated parties. The internal contracts negotiated in these countries lack strict enforcement; indeed, failure of one party to perform may leave the other party with no remedy but to honour the contract nonetheless.

The difference between a market and a managerial ethic is reflected in treatment of the savings that accrue from increased efficiency. Each country has to decide whether agencies should retain a portion or all of the savings or should remit them to the government by lowering their resource base. Considering the issue from a managerial perspective would probably lead to the conclusion that there would be significant advantage in allowing the agency to benefit from the savings. Taking away the dividend would penalise managers for being efficient, while allowing them to keep it would provide an incentive to seek further efficiencies. Inspired by its market orientation, New Zealand has come to a different conclusion. Allowing agencies to keep the saved resources would enable them to spend on services that were not contracted for in the budget. It would almost be equivalent to paying more for goods even though the price has dropped.

This example points to a critical difference between private and simulated markets. Private markets charge prices; government-induced markets pay costs. When prices are set by markets, suppliers have a strong incentive to improve efficiency; when prices are set at cost, the incentive is weak or non-existent. This inherent difference between markets and governments strongly suggests the desirability of supplementing market discipline with managerial incentives in the public sector.

Marketising public management tests the boundaries of the public sector. If government services can be fairly and efficiently supplied by commercial vendors, then one may question whether these services are so distinctive that they must remain in the public sector. Three of the countries (Australia, France, and Sweden) prefer the public delivery of government services. Except for state enterprises that already operate on a commercial basis, they generally prefer that public services be the responsibility of civil servants working in government agencies. The British government has primed various services for privatisation or contracting out, but it has not carried this development as far as some fear it might and others believe it should. New Zealand is an unusual case, for it has high regard for public institutions, but it has gone further than any other country in adapting market practices to public management. Thus far, its unique amalgam of public and market behaviour has worked rather well, but tensions may emerge in the future.

Market principles have influenced management reform in many countries. This influence is reflected in the emphasis on considering recipients of public services as customers, not as clients. Customers have power, clients do not; customers can take their business elsewhere, clients cannot. Being a customer is also different from being a citizen. Customers are more efficacious than citizens, for though the latter have rights, their interests may be ignored. The recourse provided by the voting booth pales by comparison with that available in the marketplace. The difference between citizens and customers is not only metaphorical; it is the difference between classical public administration that values uniformity and fairness in the provision of services and the new managerialism that values responsiveness to the demands of customers. It is also the difference between regarding government as a provider of services and regarding it as the architect or guardian of a good society. These differences lead to others, between a concern for outputs (the volume of goods and services provided) and a concern for outcomes (the social conditions resulting from government action). It is of some interest that although the United Kingdom's Citizen's Charter refers to citizens, the principles it enunciates value them as customers. A customer-oriented government is a service state. Its performance can be objectively measured in terms of the efficiency with which it produces output and subjectively in terms of the extent to which customers express satisfaction with the services they receive. None of the governments has narrowed its interest to customer concerns alone; all have taken a much broader view of the public interest, as reflected in efforts to measure outcomes, improve policies and programmes, evaluate results, and place their budgets on a sounder financial footing. All, however, have learned that it is much easier to improve services to customers than to address the larger role of the state in society.

DECOUPLED VERSUS CONSOLIDATED GOVERNMENT

The different perspectives of the role and performance of government clash on one of the important planks in the reform agenda – the organisation of government. For generations it was a settled principle of public administration that common activities (those serving similar objectives of clients) should be consolidated in a single organisation. Departmentalisation was seen as having many benefits, not the least of which were a narrower span of control and the synergy made possible by grouping complementary programmes together. The establishment of consolidated departments was long regarded as one of the triumphs of modern public administration. Sweden was different, for it favoured a multiplicity of separated agencies. Departmentalisation was associated with other administrative reforms, such as establishment of a comprehensive budget process, a national civil service, and the capacity to establish priorities within each sector. The costs of consolidation included a vast apparatus at the centre of departments and the layering of bureaucratic organisations, but these were deemed acceptable because they strengthened the ability of the government to co-ordinate and control the making and implementation of public policy.

Australia still endorses this administrative model, as reflected in its move to megadepartments and portfolio budgeting. In the Australian view, large, encompassing departments facilitate the establishment of objectives and priorities within portfolios. Commingling policymaking and service delivery in the same organisation permits ideas and insights derived from one of these activities to enrich the other. For example, the experiences of line managers in providing services may enable policymakers to better understand the impacts of their programmes. In the course of doing their job, these managers may gain insight into why some approaches produce the desired outcomes while others do not. In the Australian view, quarantining service providers in a separate organisation, while preoccupying them with outputs and disregarding what they may know about outcomes, would rob the government of vital performance information that can feed back into policy evaluation. It should be noted, however, that the 1996 Commission of Audit urges the separation of service delivery from policymaking. It is possible, therefore, that Australia will join the ranks of countries that have decoupled policy and management.

The integrated model has been challenged by a concept emerging out of a branch of economics known as principal-agent theory. This contemporary theory argues that principals (for example, those making policy at the centre of government) may not be able to effectively control or monitor the performance of agents (for example, those who implement the policies in operating units) because the latter have their own interests and the costs of ensuring compliance are likely to be quite high. Those who argue this position believe it likely that government policy will be captured by service providers who have informational advantages – they know more about the services than do those who make the policies. The solution devised by reformers attuned to this theory is to decouple agents from principals and to narrowly define the task assigned service agencies so as to facilitate the monitoring of the policies that providers are mandated to carry out. Application of this line of reasoning has led to the proliferation of single-purpose agencies, such as those established pursuant to the Next Steps initiative in the United Kingdom.

Theory aside, there is a strong basis for concluding that decoupling agencies from departments has boosted the awareness of service managers that they are indeed in charge, that they are not just one link in a long chain of command, and they have the means and opportunity to shape their agency to be a productive, performance-driven organisation. In visits to decoupled agencies in New Zealand and the United Kingdom, this writer sensed a new excitement that was not present in other well-run organisations. It was as if these agencies were given a fresh lease on life and empowered to make their own way with the resources and policy directives given to them.

Decoupled agencies are animated by a fresh sense of purpose, an awareness that they are not quite the same entities they were prior to being separated from their parent departments. They produce their own business plans and annual reports, they keep their own books and publish financial statements, they set performance targets and establish service standards. Each has its own chief executive and organisational identity. Quite a few have used their new authority to re-examine missions and working methods, and some have re-engineered the way they operate. Much of this vigour undoubtedly is due to the newness and fanfare of being launched as a distinct agency. At some time, the newness and excitement will fade away, and each agency will simply be a production unit in a vast state apparatus. It will be at that point that the efficiency, morale and advantages of separateness will be open to examination.

In addition to liberating and energising agencies, decoupling aims at shaking up departments and streamlining their operations. When agencies are split off, the argument runs, the parent departments should concentrate on policy guidance rather than service delivery. Their staff should be pruned and delayered, and operating responsibility should devolve to the agencies. Perhaps because it is a small country, New Zealand has had greater success in refocusing departments than has the United Kingdom. In both countries, however, the expectation that the two entities will have an arm's length relationship, in which the department will bargain hard to get more output at lower cost from its agencies, has proven to be somewhat unrealistic. When an agency is the only (or preponderant) supplier of the department's output, the two sides tend to develop an accommodating rather than a contestable relationship. The volume and price of the goods or services contracted for will be significantly influenced by what the agency believes is achievable and by what the department has to spend. Typically, it will not be a case of one side dictating terms to the other under the threat of purchasing the goods and services from an alternative source. The two entities also are likely to be interdependent as regards policy advice. Agencies have an interest in the direction that policy is taking, and departments have a need for the information and insights gleaned by their agencies in the course of providing services.

Several issues have been raised concerning the reliance on decoupled agencies for services and resources. These are set forth below in the form of questions because they cannot be resolved with the evidence and experience accumulated thus far.

- Does the agency format narrowly emphasise efficiency and outputs at the expense of effectiveness and outcomes?

- Do agencies ignore the collective interest, and thereby pose political risk to the government?

- Is the provision of public services unduly fragmented among disconnected or competitive agencies, each doing its own thing without strong co-ordination from the centre?

- Do ministries or departments have a sufficient capacity for making informed policy and monitoring performance?

- Does the establishment of independent agencies undermine traditional public service values and impede mobility of civil servants within government?

- Does the operational independence of departments threaten the doctrine of ministerial accountability?

France and Australia have opted for devolution as an alternative to decoupling. The operating units observed in Australia appear to enjoy much of the independence found in decoupled agencies, and they have taken active responsibility for developing and carrying out a work programme, and for spending and reporting on financial resources. These units are responsible for social security and taxation, two governmental functions that have well-established field offices and highly value uniformity and consistency in performing assigned tasks. These characteristics may allow more successful devolution than in organisations that have more diversified responsibilities. The French situation varies among ministries, with substantial progress on devolution in some but hardly any in others. But as additional ministries move in this direction, it may be possible to gain the benefits of agency status without incurring some of the risks.

FLEXIBILITY AND PERFORMANCE

Regardless of the form of organisation, the key issue is the extent to which operating units apply the new flexibility given to them to improve the efficiency and effectiveness of services. The basic flexibility pertains to shifting funds among items of expenditure and between fiscal years. Each country (except for France) allows almost complete discretion in spending within cash limits on running costs. The main restrictions pertain to the number and remuneration of senior officials. France still maintains separate controls on personnel, but these may be eased as reform progresses. This writer has not heard any complaints of abuse of spending discretion by departments or agencies. Some concern has been expressed that funds would be wasted if each administrative unit (such as a branch or division of a local agency) were given control of its own budget. In some cases, the finance ministry has urged fuller devolution while headquarters staff in spending departments have taken a more cautious approach, pointing to the lack of management skill and experience in individual units and to the inefficiencies of scale that might result from allowing each unit to spend as it wishes.

Shifts between fiscal years have been liberalised by permitting agencies to carry over unused funds and to pre-spend a portion of the next year's budget. Typically, the amount that may be carried forward or pre-spent is limited to a certain percentage of appropriated funds. These limits guard against hoarding of funds at a rate that would jeopardise the capacity of central agencies to control future spending. The new arrangements combine annual appropriations control and multi-year flexibility in implementing the budget. In several countries, spending flexibility is regulated by allowing agencies to earn interest on funds carried forward and charging interest on pre-spent funds.

Entrusting managers with responsibility for their operating resources has not compromised spending control. It has proven easier to maintain cash limits when managers are given a fixed budget within which to operate than when spending details are controlled by outsiders. Managers have demonstrated that they can maintain timely and accurate financial records and that they can compile financial statements that comply with accounting standards. Some countries (New Zealand and Sweden) are confident that spending units can responsibly manage their cash and they are moving to increase the role of these units in disbursing funds and maintaining their own bank accounts. Some problems have been encountered at lower managerial levels, where experience and technical skills are more limited. The French solution has been to devolve managerial responsibility at the pace that responsibility centres (or other devolved units) demonstrate capacity to follow the rules and prudently use their resources. The budget ministry has devised a formal rating system for measuring the readiness of a local unit to assume responsibility for its resources.

Flexibility in using resources is linked in every country to increased accountability for financial and operating results. Each country has introduced new instruments for compiling performance information and reporting on results. New Zealand relies on contracts between agencies and ministries; France builds performance measures into contracts between responsibility centres and ministries. In Sweden and Australia, departments and agencies compare planned and actual performance in annual reports. The United Kingdom requires Next Steps agencies to negotiate key performance targets with their departments, with results succinctly displayed in the government's annual Next Steps report.

Although there has been a significant upsurge in the volume of performance indicators, the impact of this information on managerial behaviour is less certain. The British government has had substantial success because it deliberately targets a small number of measures and publicises them in prominent reports. Australia has taken a different tack, encouraging departments to measure or describe the full array of outputs and outcomes that pertain to their programmes. But although Commonwealth departments generate and produce vast quantities of performance information every year, the impact of this material on programme and management decisions is limited. New Zealand specifies output targets in purchase agreements, but it has made less progress in measuring and monitoring outcomes.

In theory, the budget should be one of the principal means by which performance measures affect public policy. It should not be difficult to devise a performance-based budget system in which each increment of resources is directly linked to a planned increment in output. (It is not practicable, however, to directly link resources and outcomes.) Yet the governments examined here have not closely linked performance and budgeted resources, preferring instead an arrangement in which data on actual or expected results is just one of several influences on the budget. New Zealand has forged the closest link: it budgets and appropriates by object class rather than by items of expenditure, and it provides for planned outputs to be specified in purchase agreements between agencies and ministries. However, each output class typically consists of multiple performance measures, so that it is not easy to determine the portion of an appropriation allocated for the production of particular outputs. Australia and Sweden have shifted the bulk of performance information from budget documents to annual reports, thereby concentrating attention on actual rather than planned performance. The expectation is that past results will feed into future budget decisions, but neither government formally allocates resources on the basis of performance. In the United Kingdom, each department now publishes its own public expenditure report; these documents contain a considerable amount of performance information, but the direct impact on the budget may be more apparent than real.

The current wave of reforms is aimed at changing managerial behaviour, not just at rationalising budget choice. Managers – not budget makers – are intended to be the prime users of performance information. There is some apprehension that if resources were allocated on the basis of performance, the quality of the information might degrade because managers would be reluctant to produce data that would be used against them at budget time. Budget officials want performance measures, along with other information, to be available when they allocate resources. They also want a strong role in prodding departments and agencies to improve performance and to implement new accountability methods. But they do not believe that the state-of-the-art performance measurement is sufficiently advanced to justify an explicit cause-effect linkage of resources and results.

ACCOUNTING AND AUDITING

If the relationship of budgets and results is relatively loose, though somewhat closer than it once was, the measurement of performance is taking on increased prominence in financial management through the overhaul of accounting systems and the extension of audit requirements to agency financial statements and annual reports. This development is proceeding in several stages. One is a shift from cash-based to accrual accounting, a second is the requirement that departments and agencies maintain their own financial accounts and publish annual financial statements and reports, a third is the comparison of planned and actual performance, and a final stage is the audit of financial and performance statements. In some countries (New Zealand and the United Kingdom) the accounting reforms have been extended to the budget; in others (Australia and

Sweden) they have not. However, recent developments indicate that Australia will also apply accounting standards to the budget.

Accrual accounting has been implemented in New Zealand and is being introduced in Australia and the United Kingdom. The governments moving in this direction have accepted the principle that commercial standards should be applied except when they do not suit the operations of public entities. The accounting reforms are seen as an important part of the process of transforming spenders into managers. Those who manage public money must be accountable for costs. They must know the full resources expended and they must control those costs. The logic of accrual accounting requires that operating units be charged for the cost of the accommodations they occupy, the assets they use, and (in some cases) the indirect costs of operations. Two conditions must prevail for accrual accounting to be more than a bookkeeping exercise: managers must have genuine choice in deciding whether to bear the costs; and the costs they are charged must have an impact on the financial resources available to them. If, for example, managers were charged for government-supplied accommodations, they should have the option of relocating to other premises. If they lack real choice, and must use assigned space and pay whatever is charged, full cost accounting would be counterproductive. Rather than empowering managers to take responsibility for costs, it would tell them that they are powerless to run their own operations.

The second condition is that costs affect the resources available to the agency. If an agency were charged for depreciation, this cost should reduce the resources otherwise available for operations. In New Zealand, for example, the capital charge levied on the net assets of departments is part of each agency's operating costs; the higher this charge, the less money is available for other expenditures. Controlling costs in this manner suggests that accrual basis be extended to budgeting and not be limited to financial reporting. New Zealand has already moved in this direction, and the United Kingdom has announced its intention to do so. It is worth noting that when the budget is placed on an accrual basis, expenditure is still controlled on a cash basis. Thus, the United Kingdom intends to maintain cash limits on running costs after accrual methods are introduced.

Although accrual accounting and budgeting requires some start-up investment in training and information systems, agencies studied for this report indicate that they have had little difficulty making the switch. But in many cases, agencies see this merely as a technical requirement rather than as a management tool. Some are using accrual accounting to facilitate full-cost recovery through user charges or efficiency improvements through the measurement of unit costs. In the future, one can envision using the new accounting systems to budget on the basis of marginal (rather than average) costs, to distinguish between fixed and variable costs in resource allocation, to compare lease or buy options, to establish the actual cost of loans or guarantees issued by the government, to measure the incremental cost of incremental output, to determine benchmark or standard costs, to analyse the variance between planned and actual costs or performance, and so on. To do these things, governments will have to greatly improve their competence in cost allocation and analysis, which is a different way of looking at budgets than standard expenditure computations.

Financial statements, prepared according to accepted accounting principles, are rapidly becoming standard features in department and agency annual reports. The array of financial statements is similar to that found in commercial organisations. Agencies indicate that they have had relatively little difficulty in compiling the data, but they do not generally make much use of these statements in internal management. As in the business sector, these statements satisfy external reporting requirements. It may be that the greatest value of these financial reports is the process of preparing them. To compile financial statements, agencies must maintain timely and accurate accounts and they must be informed on the condition of their assets and liabilities. In every country, there has been a marked increase in the accounting responsibility placed on departments and agencies. In several, it no longer suffices for the Treasury to publish a combined statement for the government; spending units have to keep their own books.

Annual reports also contain an increasing amount of performance information. This portion of the report is not as standardised as the financial statements, and probably never will be. At present, much of the performance information is descriptive; agencies use the annual report to enumerate many of the things they did during the year. As annual reports take on more importance, as they have in New Zealand, Sweden and Australia, agencies will be required to present a more systematic comparison of actual against planned performance. This requirement may be enforced by subjecting both the financial statements and performance information to audit. Sweden has already taken this step; it has given the National Audit Office broad scope to review the annual reports of all agencies and to qualify those reports that have material shortcomings. This role fits easily into the Swedish system because the audit office is under the jurisdiction of the Ministry of Finance. In other countries, however, the audit office is accountable to parliament, so that aggressive review of annual reports or of other documents sometimes generates tension between it and the finance ministry. In Australia, Department of Finance officials have been wary that an active role by the audit office in reviewing programme evaluations and performance information might dampen the willingness of managers to take a hard look at their operations. Nevertheless, the trend is unmistakably in the direction of broadening the role of auditors in reviewing statements made by government agencies concerning their performance.

POLICIES AND PROGRAMMES

In the OECD community, running costs typically account for less than 20 per cent of central government expenditure. A much larger share of the budget is spent on programmes – transfers to households, subsidies to businesses, grants to other governments and other programme expenditures. These expenditures have been rising much more rapidly than running costs, and are much more rigid. It would be wasted opportunity if administrative operations were modernised, but the methods by which programmes were selected, implemented and carried out were unchanged. In fact, most of the governments reviewed here regard enhanced programme effectiveness as a key objective of reform. Yet few of the innovations discussed thus far would have much impact on the mix or effectiveness of government programmes, or on the amount spent on them. The logic of restructuring assumes that well-run organisations will re-examine programme cost and performance, but there is little evidence that this expectation has been realised.

In a fundamental sense, what government does – its objectives and policies, and the priorities and programmes it spends money on – are political, not management, issues. Performance information and the other instruments discussed above can influence policy and programme decisions, but they are rarely the only or most important influences. Moreover, these decisions cannot be routinised in ways that administrative operations often are. Political and policy actions tend to be opportunistic, taken according to no fixed schedule but on the impulse of political leaders when conditions are deemed right. For this reason, the episodic activities of Swedish study committees may have greater impact on public policy than does the scheduled evaluation of programmes such as occurs in Australia. For generations, the British government has issued major policy pronouncements in White Papers that are published when the government sees fit to do so. These are not published according to any fixed schedule, but they often influence ensuing policies.

Several countries have sought to rationalise government programmes and policies through strategic planning, outcome measures and programme evaluation. Strategic planning is the most ambitious of these instruments. It differs from conventional planning in that the object is not merely to change programmes but to transform the organisation itself. The key questions raised in a strategic review pertain to what the organisation should be, not simply to what it should do. This type of question is most likely to elicit a strategic review when new agencies are launched, as in New Zealand and the United Kingdom. The process of defining what the new organisation should be helps build group identification and enables the agency to project itself as a transformed entity. Once the agency is an ongoing operation, its annual business or operating plan might be more relevant for management decisions than would the longer-range strategic outlook.

Strategic planning has much fuller application in business than in government. The most important strategic decision for a business is whether to enter or exit a particular market; whether, for example, to remain a typewriter company or to abandon that line of business and become an information processing company instead. In government, fundamental decisions on whether an agency should operate a particular programme are made through the political process, not by public agencies. Yet strategic planning can facilitate change by an agency when conditions are supportive. In New Zealand, for example, the Customs Department has been largely transformed from an organisation that interdicted illegal goods and enforced tariffs to one that facilitates international trade. In this case, department leaders suggested that the change was expedited and legitimised by strategic planning, but would have occurred in due course without the strategic exercise. This transformation, which has occurred in the customs operations of other countries as well, points to strategic planning as an opportunistic rather than a routinised activity.

The reform agenda has two principal means of changing programmes – outcome measures that feedback to programme decisions and periodic evaluations. The former typically are compiled annually, the latter require a longer time frame. In every country, the government has encountered considerably more difficulty measuring outcomes than outputs. Measuring outcomes is not a temporary or transitional problem; it will not be solved by installing better performance information systems. It has not been solved in New Zealand by making ministers responsible for outcomes, or in Australia by investing heavily in programme evaluation, or in the United Kingdom by targeting a few key measures, or in Sweden by investing in effectiveness audits. It certainly will not be solved by incorporating these measures in annual budget exercises. Outcomes are difficult to measure and apply because they relate to matters beyond the direct control of the responsible agency. Outcomes measure social conditions, not only organisational performance.

Although governments may not cause outcomes, they must be aware of them. Outcome measures are directional signals that tell an agency whether it is getting closer to or further away from vital social objectives, not because the agency is to be blamed or credited for the results but because it should know whether its programmes are accomplishing what is intended. Outcomes are strategic measures that spur an agency to question what it is doing and where it is heading. An agency should have only a few strategic measures; too many would dim the signal and might have a paralysing impact. It should not be hard to define a few such measures. They relate to the essence of the agency, the reason(s) why it exists and carries out particular programmes. In selecting such measures, an agency would do well to be guided by its answer to the following questions: why do we exist at all, and how do we know whether we are succeeding or not?

These are strategic questions; like strategic planning they focus on the organisation itself rather than on the things it does. Yet there also is ample room for assessing programmes in the light of the objectives set for them. Australia has gone further than any country in injecting evaluation into the stream of policy and budget decisions, but it has discovered how much easier it is to conduct evaluations than to use them in making decisions. Efforts to increase the use of evaluations run up against two problems. One is the anomaly that the influence of evaluations on government actions rises when they are integrated into decisional cycles, such as annual budget formulation, but that routinised evaluations tend to lack depth and they therefore are less likely to disturb the prevailing allocation of resources of mix and programmes. Second, the culture of evaluation is one that looks for means of improving programmes by finding shortcomings in existing operations. Evaluation is not likely to be long supported by government if it habitually finds failure in government. Programme evaluation operates at the intersection of politics and management. It challenges both the objectives of government and the assumptions of programmes. For this reason alone, it is more difficult to institutionalise than most other items on the reform agenda. The stakes are higher and the political risks greater.

PATHWAYS TO REFORM

There are many roads to reform of the public sector. When a country embarks on restructuring public management, it must take a path that is compatible with its political and governmental conditions. What works or is acceptable in one country might not be in another. The threshold question for the many OECD Member countries that have not sought to fundamentally change management practices is whether they should start down this path at all. Why, in the light of the problems encountered by the countries examined in this report, should any other country make the enormous investment in reforming public management? Why should political leaders try to change the managing culture of government departments when the task will take a decade or more to complete, and when the payoffs in better public services will take some time to materialise?

Contemporary management reform has been driven less by political logic than by budget pressures and a sense that public institutions have become outmoded and inefficient. Undoubtedly, management reform in the public sector has been influenced by parallel developments in business management, but the greatest influence has come from awareness of the need to do more with less. Politicians can curry some voter approval by projecting a modern, reformist image. But the search for votes has not been the main motivating force, nor is it likely to be in the future. In fact, politicians risk being punished by voters if reform is perceived as dismantling the modern state or weakening its capacity to perform. The Labour Party paid a price at the polls in New Zealand in national

29

elections following its bold reform of the public sector. Reformist governments also have been replaced in France and Sweden, though the management changes probably had little to do with the election results in these countries.

In each of the countries surveyed here, public sector restructuring has survived a change in government. In every case, the successor government has built on the reforms already under way and has deepened or extended them. In the United Kingdom, the Financial Management Initiative was broadened by Next Steps; in France, the Rocard Initiative was reinforced by Prime Minister Juppe's circular which converted the responsibility centres from pilot tests to national policy; in Sweden, the triennial budget frames introduced by the Social Democratic government were implemented by the centre-right coalition that succeeded it; in New Zealand, a Labour government enacted pioneering reforms that were subsequently endorsed and broadened by the National government; and in Australia, the 1996 change of government was followed by an Audit Commission that applauded previous initiatives such as the forward estimates, evaluation strategy and running costs regime and proposed some additional innovations. In all of the study countries, formal assessments sponsored by the government came to the conclusion that the reforms have had a positive impact on public management. In none of the countries did the assessment call for a return to the old ways.

The assessments offered in this report say more about changes in procedure than about changes in behaviour. Yet the true payoff in government restructuring comes from the latter. Because the assessments have been made while restructuring has been under way – it has not yet been completed in any of the countries – they do not provide a final judgement of the sustainability of the reforms. There is reason to expect that sooner or later reform runs out of steam, perhaps because the government's interest or agenda turns to other matters, perhaps because the core ideas and standards of public management change. Some aspects of reform are likely to be subject to political controversy, particularly the fragmentation of the civil service and the contracting out of core government functions. Nevertheless, judging from the length of time that governments in the five countries have persisted with efforts to modernise public management, we can expect important changes to endure. If they do, contemporary governments should have more efficient public sectors, though not necessarily more positive programme outcomes. There is considerable evidence of efficiency gains resulting from decreases in staffing levels and forced reductions in operating expenditures, but none of the countries has yet undertaken a systematic examination of programme results to determine whether and how they have been affected by the changes under way. The countries are laboratories of new management practices. They provide the OECD community with a rich menu of possibilities for coping with fiscal stress, upgrading public sector efficiency, improving the quality of services and responsiveness to customers, and changing the operating culture of government departments and agencies. There is much to be learned from their experiences, and many new possibilities for organising work and delivering services have been opened. Now is one of the truly exciting periods in the evolution of public management. But there also are many questions to be asked. Governments bent on reforming management practices must seek their own answers.

The process of reform

One of the first choices for restructuring governments is whether to proceed on an across-the-board basis or in a more piecemeal and gradual manner. Should prospective innovations be pilot-tested first, as they were in Sweden, or imposed in advance, as they were in New Zealand? Pilot tests have the obvious advantage of enabling the government to build support for the reform, garner some experience, and make adjustments before the changes are fully launched. But there also is the risk that pilot-testing will dissipate interest and support before the reforms have been institutionalised. Moreover, because it is conducted under experimental conditions, a pilot may not be a true test of how a reform will operate when it is fully implemented. Despite extensive advance testing, Sweden found that a fixed three-year cycle was unduly rigid and was not appropriate for all agencies. On the other hand, implementing the reforms through political (or management) blitzkrieg might bring quick results but increase the need for major adjustments as experience accumulates. This has been the case in New Zealand, which has been compelled to add many features that were not contemplated when the reforms were initiated. In view of the far-reaching nature of the reforms, it is likely that adjustments will have to be made along the way, regardless of the manner in which they are introduced.

With the five models examined here, governments might experiment with more than one type of reform. They might try to "mix and match" elements from different countries; for example, Australia's evaluation strategy with New Zealand's output measures and purchase agreements, or France's responsibility centres with Sweden's multi-year budget frames. The problem, however, is that the more varied and complex a management system is, the more costly it is to manage. The new managerial regime imposes substantial informational demands on departments; governments must guard against overburdening their administrative organs by melding together requirements from different management systems.

Management reform generally has been an amalgam of top-down guidance and bottom-up implementation. Without impetus from the top, reform is not likely to get off the ground, and even if it does, implementation will be uneven. France decentralised reform by enabling ministries to innovate as they saw fit.

Some ministries enthusiastically embraced reform, while others only went through the motions and made few genuine changes. New Zealand, by contrast, took a highly centralised approach that blanketed the entire state sector with uniform rules and requirements. Its approach might not be easily transplanted to larger, more diverse political systems. At some point, managers must be brought into the process; they must feel that the reforms are workable and that their concerns are being addressed. If they are not, managers may subvert the reforms – usually not by opposing change but by being indifferent to it. Changing the culture of management cannot happen without changing the behaviour of managers.

Regardless of the approach taken, reform will not be quick or easy. A country considering an overhaul of public management faces a decade or more of innovation and experimentation and is likely to move in directions that were not foreseen when the reforms were initiated.

Governmental organisation

In each of the countries, restructuring has been targeted at the processes by which decisions are taken, resources are managed, information is gathered and reported, and ministers and officials are held to account for what they have done and accomplished. In Australia and Sweden, these changes have taken place within pre-existing organisational structures; in the other countries, the creation of new organisations has been an important "driver" of reform. Australia has not established new organisations, though it did reorganise departments within broad ministerial portfolios. As noted earlier, the government that took office in 1996 may decide to separate service-delivery agencies from policymaking departments. Sweden has found no need to reorganise because its governmental structure defines the roles of ministries and agencies.

Can management be reformed within conventional or pre-existing organisations? The answer depends on the objectives of reorganisation. If, as often was the case in the past, organisational responsibilities are shifted among departments to shake things up by disturbing existing arrangements, then reorganisation is not likely to have much impact on performance. This type of reorganisation no longer is in vogue; it is generally recognised that the unintended effects may outweigh the intended ones. If, however, administrative responsibilities are rearranged to make agents (service providers) accountable to principals (ministers or top managers), then the reorganisation can fundamentally alter organisational performance.

In all of the countries (assuming Australia moves to decouple service delivery) there is a formal demarcation between policy and service. Is this distinction tenable? Does it clarify roles and responsibilities, or does it muddle accountability by ignoring the interdependence of policy and administration? There is no doubt that the roles can be formally differentiated; the question is whether the formal distinctions hold up in practice. In several decoupled countries, three layers of government have emerged: the ministerial level at which political responsibility is lodged; the department which exercises managerial responsibility on behalf of the government; and the delivery agencies which are responsible for providing the services. Inevitably, problems have emerged in relations among the entities. When there is a breakdown in services or a failure to perform, is it a political or managerial responsibility? Are the policymakers at fault or those managers who have failed to perform as expected?

When several entities share responsibility, difficulties may emerge in their relationships and in enforcing accountability. Some matters will fall between the cracks of the accountability system. In the United Kingdom, for example, the relationship between agency chief executives and departmental permanent secretaries requires clarification. New Zealand has experienced some difficulty in sorting out the respective responsibilities of ministers and chief executives. In these and other countries, a period of adjustment may be needed before the new roles are fully institutionalised, devolution takes root, and understandings are forged. But more than settling in may be required to work out differences in perspectives. Do the new relationships invite protracted tension and misunderstanding? Can contractual arrangements, such as framework documents and performance or purchase agreements, establish trust between policymakers and managers or compensate for the lack of trust? Is there an inherent contradiction between the doctrine and expectations of devolution on the one hand and the responsibilities of elected politicians and senior managers on the other? What is the appropriate distribution of risk among the various entities and levels? Is it feasible in democratic regimes to wall off political risk from managerial discretion? The urgency of these questions is largely a function of the organisational changes under way. The issue is less troubling in Sweden, where the separation of ministries and agencies is well established, than in New Zealand and the United Kingdom, where long-standing doctrines of ministerial accountability have been challenged.

In all of the countries, restructuring has strained relations between central agencies and line departments. The expectation of managers that they will be free to spend as they will and to operate their agencies without central interference clashes with the ongoing responsibility of central agencies for legality, efficiency and effectiveness in public expenditure. In reforming public management, it is much easier to specify what central agencies should stop doing than to decide what they should continue (or start) to do. Questions that must be resolved in sorting out the respective roles include: What is the proper division of responsibility between the finance ministry (or similar organisation) and spending departments? How are disputes between the two to be resolved when the spenders feel that central intervention infringes on their managerial discretion, and the central agencies feel that failure to intervene would weaken financial control? When is central guidance appropriate, or even essential, and when is it meddlesome? What should the central agency do when it detects inadequate capacity (or will) in newly independent departments to manage their own operations? What should be the balance between advising and prodding, between encouraging agencies to get on with the task of managing their affairs and intervening when they are not up to the task? The answers will differ from country to country, but in none can post-reform public management abandon central oversight and guidance.

Management reform has uncluttered budgeting from many of the details of expenditure. The expectation was that budget offices would thereby be freed up to work on larger strategic and policy issues: the control of total expenditure and programme innovation. In some models, the budget was to become the central organ for strategic management in government, prodding departments and agencies to adopt the reforms and change their operating methods. This model portends a fundamental transformation in the role of the finance ministry (or similar organ) from a controlling organisation into a leader of management reform. This transformation clearly is under way in Australia, New Zealand and the United Kingdom, though the affected agencies do not always acknowledge the extent to which their relationship with the budget organisation has been altered. Change is less pronounced in Sweden, but only because the Ministry of Finance has always been relatively small. There is evidence of change in the French budget ministry, but it will probably be another few years before the full impact of modernisation is felt.

What would a transformed budget organisation be? During the "reform" period, budget officials do not have to face this question because they are busy with transitional work, getting rid of old rules and prodding agencies to adopt new methods. But once reform has been normalised, the budget office will have to reflect on how it fits into the operations of government, which controls it is to maintain, what levers it must have to induce recalcitrant agencies to produce. In a culture of management that professes to value devolution, defining a useful role for central departments is not an easy task. The British Treasury has tackled this question in a fundamental review that has produced a smaller, delayered organisation. Other governments can be expected to consider the issue in the years ahead.

In much of the reform literature, the relationship between central organs, such as finance, and the operating departments is portrayed in confusing terms. The role of the centre, it is said, is to assist but not intervene, to make strategic decisions but not the everyday ones, to control total spending but not the particulars, to devise new management methods but not to impose them, to encourage the measurement of results but not to allocate on the basis of results, to push for efficiencies but not to capture (for the government) the financial benefits of efficiency, to speak for devolution but to allow each department to devolve in its own way. Other mixed messages can be added to this list, but the point is obvious to any budget official who has wondered why the finance ministry is not applauded for the strides it has already taken. Budgeting in the future will be a difficult balancing act, for it will have to reconcile the conflicting roles and responsibilities ascribed to the budget office.

In sorting out its future niche, the budget organisation will be pulled in two directions. One is for budgeting to become integrated into financial management through closer links with accounting and auditing, cost and output measurement, management information systems, and other management routines. The other direction is to become the policymaking centre of government, to be at the frontier of programme development and strategic thinking. On paper, the two roles can be harmonised. In fact, Australia has vigorously sought to integrate both roles: to build budgeting into the routines of financial management as well as into the opportunities for policy innovation. This combined role is the ideal, for the regularities of budgeting make an excellent instrument of financial management while the decision-impelling characteristics of budgeting make it an excellent instrument of strategic choice. Packaging the two roles in the same organisation will not be an easy task, however.

Means of accountability

Although accountability is a key element of reform in all of the countries, the means of securing it differ. The United Kingdom has taken the position that true accountability lies in turning over as much as possible to the market, either by privatisation or contracting out. This determination to extend the boundaries of the market to the public sector implies little confidence in the conventional means sought in Australia. New Zealand also seeks to inject market discipline into the public sector, but does so by recasting the budget into a contract for specified output. France takes a different approach, relying on the commitment of public managers to perform well, while Sweden seeks to enhance accountability by relying on the division of labour between ministries and agencies. The selection of instruments depends on the objectives sought by the government. If the aim is to significantly slow the growth rate of public expenditure, then restructuring is likely to rely on market-type mechanisms. If, however, the principal objective is to improve efficiency in public expenditure, then decentralised management combined with an emphasis on performance measurement might be preferred.

In one way or another, all the countries place some weight on the measurement of performance. They do so either because it is a vital feature of the accountability framework or because these measures substitute (if only weakly) for markets. Reliance on performance measurement opens the door to practical questions which reform-minded governments must face. Who should have the last word in selecting the appropriate measures? Is it preferable to devise a large number of measures that cover the range of activities or outputs, or would it be better to concentrate on a few, even if this entails neglecting certain aspects of performance? How does one wean agencies away from process and efficiency measures and toward those that address outcomes and results? What should be the link between output and outcome measures? What, if anything, should governments do to avert distortions in behaviour resulting from the use of measures as official targets?

The foregoing questions pertain to the development of measures. Additional questions arise concerning their use. By itself, measuring performance changes little or nothing. What matters are the steps taken after the data are gathered. To what extent should performance data be audited to assure accuracy? What interventions should be made in case performance falls short of the target? What should be the role of Parliament in reviewing performance and initiating corrective actions? How should the measures be enforced through performance agreements or other procedures?

Linkage of performance measures to budget allocations

New Zealand and France may be at opposite poles in relating performance data and other management changes to budget policy. The former expressly links budgets and performance; it makes appropriations by output classes. The French seem wary of coupling budget policy and performance, preferring instead to have budget allocations reflect the government's policies and priorities. The tighter the relationship between budgets and performance, the greater the need for cost accounting methods that allocate the full cost of services to outputs. Given the primitive state of cost accounting in many countries, full cost attribution is not currently feasible.

The progressive introduction of business accounting practices – such as accrual accounting – into the public sector should make it feasible to base budget decisions on performance information. Nevertheless, questions may be raised concerning the implications of this trend. Should managers be charged for costs over which they lack effective control? For example, does it serve managerial accountability to charge managers for space occupied in government-owned buildings when they must use the assigned accommodations? What gain is there in allocating overhead or other costs that are outside the manager's discretion?

Ideally, the use of commercial-type accounting should keep pace with the expansion of managerial discretion, but this ideal may be difficult to translate into concrete practice.

Finally, in considering the linkage of budgets and performance, one should not lose sight of the fact that restructuring directly touches only on operating (or running) costs, not on programme expenditures, which are much more prominent in government budgets. The logic of restructuring assumes that well-run organisations will also examine the cost and performance of the money spent on transfer payments, grants and subsidies. But the assessments provide little evidence that this expectation has been realised. When all is done, if restructuring reaches only to the internal operations of agencies, industrial democracies will enter the next century more efficiently managed but with budget crises at least as severe as those many have faced in the past two decades.

2

AUSTRALIA

Since 1984, the government has initiated more than a dozen reforms aimed at improving the management of Commonwealth departments and agencies and the effectiveness of public programmes. For convenience, the various reforms can be sorted into two broad initiatives – the Financial Management Improvement Programme (FMIP) and Programme Management and Budgeting (PMB). The FMIP cluster includes running cost arrangements, efficiency dividends, flexibility to carry over unused funds and to borrow from future budgets, devolution, performance indicators, accrual accounting and resource agreements. The PMB cluster includes forward estimates, programme budgeting, the evaluation strategy, policy work and budget decisions in the Cabinet, portfolio budgeting and megadepartments, and efforts to measure outcomes. The reforms also cover user charges and commercialisation, corporate plans, and far-reaching changes in human resource management. These categories overlap, and the various reforms are sometimes classified differently in official documents than they are here. In fact, one of the most conspicuous features of the Australian model is the commingling of managerial and policy elements. The government has refused to decouple policymaking from service implementation, insisting instead that managers and ministers alike can contribute to better policy, which is the main objective of reform. Nevertheless, there are important differences between the policymaking and management domains, and these have affected the progress of reform.

At the time the reforms were initiated in the early 1980s, Australia was experiencing considerable economic difficulty – a pesky recession, unwanted deficits and deteriorating relative economic performance. Yet the reforms were not animated by a sense of crisis or by a professed determination to reverse the course of government policy. Little was said about trimming the size of the public sector or about saving money, although there was a widely publicised policy to reduce the deficit to more manageable proportions. The public sector was to be strengthened by reform, not diminished. The 1984 *White Paper on Budget Reform* noted that the public sector contributes to economic growth "which can be drawn upon to finance public expenditure programmes". In Australia, management reform has had more to do with reallocating public resources – putting them to more effective use – than with cutting them, with getting more value for public money by spurring civil servants to do a better job.

Reform of the public sector had its origin in a widely held view that the performance of public administration had fallen below desired and acceptable levels. A 1984 diagnostic study concluded that this decline was due to rigid, detailed and overcentralised management. The study found that managers in the Australian public sector believed that they had little discretion in the use of personnel and financial resources and little opportunity or incentive to take risks or initiative. Their job was to comply with the rules. In budgeting, these rules were predicated on detailed appropriations and controls that denied managers flexibility in carrying out the programmes for which they were responsible. In response to these findings, the government issued White Papers on reforming the public sector and budget reform. The latter, which is our interest here, led to two main initiatives – the Financial Management Improvement Programme (FMIP) and Programme Management and Budgeting (PMB), along with the liberalisation of financial controls on spending departments and new instruments for holding them accountable for results. The 1984 diagnostic study summed up the basic rationale of the reforms as a shift in management emphasis from compliance to a greater degree of performance control.

Thus, reforms were inspired by findings that the public service had become sluggish and compliant, unwilling to take risks or initiative, and more concerned with upholding encrusted rules and procedures than with producing public good. The reformers were confident that once managers were freed up to manage, they would. They would reallocate resources, closely examine the quality and effectiveness of services, seek initiatives to raise productivity, and take charge of their operations. This expectation was based on the assumption that failure of managers to perform was due to constraints imposed on them rather than uncaring attitudes. The concern with human resources management is reflected in the fact that the first salvo of reforms did not pertain to budgeting or financial management but to Reforming the Australian Public Sector. This was the title of a 1983 White Paper; an almost identical title – The Australian Public Sector Reformed – was applied to a comprehensive evaluation of the reforms conducted in 1992. That assessment was based in substantial part on a survey of 10 000 civil servants. In assessing the progress of reform, the government wanted to know what its employees and managers thought about their jobs. The attitudes and behaviour of public managers was deemed more relevant in judging the success of reform than was reviewing which expenditures were folded into running costs or how various activities were classified in a programme structure.

The revitalisation of the public service could not be accomplished without the innovations in budgeting and financial management introduced by FMIP and PMB. Although these changes have affected financing arrangements, the government also has been mindful of the impact on broader aspects of the public service. It was to "reflect the wider scope of FMIP within reform in the public sector" that a parliamentary review published in 1990 was labelled Not Dollars Alone. The dollars were important, but so, too, were the commitment and competence of the public service.

There is some reason to believe that this attitude may be changing and that greater emphasis may be placed in the future on curtailing public expenditure. One portent of change has been the 1996 election of a liberal government, replacing the Labour government that had held power since 1983; another has been the June 1996 report of the National Commission of Audit which recommended major changes in Commonwealth programmes and management practices. The commission proposed that management be restructured along the lines of reforms that have been adopted in New Zealand and the United Kingdom, including separating service delivery from policymaking, preparing the budget on an accrual basis, and publishing "whole of Government" financial statements.

Although the new liberal government has looked favourably on the commission's recommendations, it is too early to determine the direction that reform will take. Accordingly, this chapter concentrates on the management practices introduced during the 1984-95 period. However, the concluding section of the chapter sets forth some of the conclusions and recommendations of the Commission of Audit and assesses their compatibility with the management changes made since 1984.

DEREGULATING PUBLIC MANAGEMENT

An essential first step in reform was eliminating the controls that blocked managerial initiative. Reform would have been stillborn if managers were mobilised to take responsibility for their actions but were then hamstrung by rules and procedures that prescribed exactly how they were to run their operations. Prior to reform, departments received separate appropriations for as many as twenty-one line items. They were restricted in shifting funds among the items, and they had to obtain advance approval of Parliament or the Department of Finance for many routine administrative matters. These controls were reinforced by detailed budget estimates and by close scrutiny of the details by parliamentary committees. From beginning to end, budgeting was riveted on inputs. What was accomplished by the money seemed of less consequence than that it was spent according to rule. The Cabinet often had to decide on relatively minor administrative details when it reviewed spending bids by departments. The tight financial controls were paralleled by central control of personnel. Changes in staffing levels or in job classifications were reviewed by the Public Service Board, even when funds were available within the budget to pay for the changes.

Departments often had to receive clearance from two central agencies to recruit staff – from Finance to ensure that money was set aside for the purpose, and from the Board to ensure that the myriad personnel rules were complied with. The compilation of financial and other management data as well as the maintenance of accounts were centralised, with departments receiving such information as others thought they needed to comply with the regulations imposed on them.

Centralised control took a heavy toll in managerial performance. A diagnostic study of the public service conducted in the early days of FMIP found that managers believed they had little discretion in using personnel and financial resources and little opportunity or incentive to take risks, even when the expected payoff was improved performance. In fact, 94 per cent of the senior managers surveyed in the diagnostic study saw financial management as little else than controlling expenditures against appropriations and spending the sum allocated. To break this pattern of control, the 1983 (Reid) *Review of Commonwealth Administration* called on the central departments to "place less emphasis on their detailed control activity. The accent should be on the periodic assessment of departmental performance to support limited day-to-day monitoring". This argument was backed up by the diagnostic study which explicitly linked progress in divesting *ex ante* controls with the strengthening of management accountability.

In seeking to revitalise the public service, Australian reformers opted for procedural rather than structural change. They did not decouple agencies from departments, nor did they establish new institutions to manage the reforms. The Public Service Board was terminated, but no dramatic restructuring was sought in the Department of Finance. The Cabinet and parliamentary committees retained an active role in budget decisions, though both were more sharply focused on priorities and performance than before. Administrative expenditure was consolidated into a single appropriation for running costs, and the three-year forward estimates were strengthened as a constraint on future expenditure. Ministers and managers were accorded considerable freedom in shifting resources to preferred uses, the former within forward estimates, the latter within cash limits on running costs. A programme structure was introduced for reporting on performance, and fresh emphasis was given to the evaluation of programmes.

As noted, these reforms were promoted under the aegis of FMIP and PMB. Throughout the reform effort, the government has perceived FMIP and PMB as having common roots and objectives. Both are riveted on performance, both encourage trade-offs and flexibility. FMIP deals mostly with operational matters, PMB with policy work. FMIP aims to let managers manage, PMB makes ministers decide. But though they share a common logic, the two sets of reform inhabit different spheres of government and are sometimes pulled in opposite directions. On many matters, such as their commitment to performance, FMIP and PMB reinforce one another. But several tensions have emerged in the past decade.

One pertains to the structure of the budget, a second to devolution of management responsibility, and the third to the role of the Department of Finance.

FMIP dictates that resources be allocated to organisational units that are accountable for their use; PMB stresses that resources be allocated on the basis of the objectives pursued by government. In the early development of the reforms, the government opted to retain an organisational structure for appropriations and it introduced a programme structure for reporting on performance. Although the two structures coexist, only one can be the basis on which resources are allocated. Only one structure can be for decisions, any other can only provide supporting information. In basing decisions on organisational units, the government relegated the programme structure to a secondary role. It has become the "fifth wheel" of Australian budgeting, a paperwork burden that adds little value to budget decisions.

FMIP emphasises devolution to line managers; PMB has spurred the concentration of policy responsibility in broad portfolios. It is no contradiction to move in both directions. Management theory and business practice suggest that strategic direction at the top is a precondition for successfully devolving operational responsibility down the line. However, the establishment of megadepartments has sometimes impeded genuine devolution. There is so much traffic in policy matters at the top – corporate and evaluation plans within portfolios, submissions to Cabinet, and an enormous flow of paper to Parliament – and so much distance between the policy echelons and service delivery that line managers cannot always see how their slice of the public service fits into the larger scheme.

Finally, FMIP has impelled the Department of Finance to withdraw from the details of expenditure management; PMB has thrust Finance into a central role in making and evaluating public programmes and policies. In design, there is no conflict between disengaging from operational matters and taking a strong role on policy issues. In practice, it is not always easy to draw the line between the two roles, nor is it easy to communicate the difference to others. What, for example, should be the role of Finance in evaluating programmes? Should it promote good evaluation practices and then allow departments to conduct their own assessments, or should it actively participate in evaluations? Finance has tried to straddle both sides of this question. It accepts that departments should own their evaluations, but it nevertheless manoeuvres to have a front seat in the process. Some managers complain that Finance gives them mixed signals, but this may be inevitable in a reform agenda that is as full and varied as FMIP and PMB.

FMIP has received the lion's share of attention over the past decade, perhaps because it is the easier to accomplish. Most of the financial management reforms have been successfully implemented, though there are ongoing adjustments in running costs and other elements of the system, and considerable work remains to be done in shifting to accrual accounting. Although one may question whether the reforms add up to a fundamental transformation in the public service, the government's thorough evaluation of FMIP and this writer's observations in Australia strongly indicate that today's managers are free to manage in ways that were unthinkable barely a dozen years ago.

The judgement must be somewhat reserved in the case of PMB. Although the forward estimates have injected discipline and structure into the policy process, the programme structure adds paper but not value, good outcome measures remain elusive, and the increased volume of evaluations has not been matched by using these findings in budget and policy decisions. In some ways the fate of PMB resembles that of programme budgeting that was tried a generation ago. (PMB was initially labelled programme budgeting when the reforms were launched in 1984.) The government has taken steps to de-emphasise the programme structure and to place more weight on evaluation work. These moves will not be the last adjustments to programme management and budgeting.

In assessing the reforms, it is useful to begin with some general conclusions and then to comment on specific elements. The transformation of the Australian public sector has been carried out through more than two dozen distinct but mutually reinforcing innovations. The cumulative impact of the reforms has been greater than that of any individual change. In the space of ten years, the official 1992 assessment concluded, agencies coped with large amounts of change that produced substantial savings and better quality service. Moreover, the new framework had strong support and was seen as having improved the long-term cost-effectiveness of the public service, including the outcomes for taxpayers and clients. As stated in the *Australian Public Sector Reformed* report:

> *Many activities in the Commonwealth public sector are being performed more efficiently and effectively than was the case, say, ten years ago. Much of this improvement is attributable to the broad suite of reforms, both individually and collectively, introduced in a progressive manner since 1983 – and the* FMIP *has been a prominent contributor.*

There have been some hitches, however. While the scope of reform has covered the entire public sector, the new culture of performance has not permeated all agencies. In some cases, managers newly empowered to act do not fully understand and accept the need for balance between accountability and freedom to manage. Because of the prominence of FMIP and resource constraints, many managers perceive restructuring as pertaining to financial management; there has been inadequate understanding of how the various reforms fit into a comprehensive overhaul of the public sector.

The impetus for change has come from the top, but the objective of the reforms has been the devolution of decision-making capacity and responsibility from higher to lower echelons in the organisation and from central units to line agencies. On paper this aim has been largely realised, but it has given rise to new strains in relations between central and operating units. Only about half of all agencies surveyed in the assessment believe that devolution has been achieved "to a great extent". Some operating agencies perceive a discrepancy between the new role of the Department of Finance as promoter of reform and its traditional role as the controller of resources. A parallel tension has arisen between letting (or making) managers manage and focusing on results, and also being prescriptive about inputs. The great majority of senior officials do not want Finance to take a strong role in controlling departmental finances.

A parallel problem has arisen concerning internal devolution within agencies from headquarters staff to programme managers. At the time of the assessment, agencies were at very different stages of internal devolution. Some large agencies had shifted most responsibilities to line managers, but in others central staff held on to the level of control. Because Australia has not decoupled operating agencies from their departments, devolution is likely to proceed at a halting, uneven pace.

FINANCIAL MANAGEMENT IMPROVEMENT

With so many innovations in play, the cumulative impact of the reforms has been greater than that of any individual reform. No single change has so transformed the public sector that it would be unrecognisable to one who last observed it before reform. The absence of a single transforming reform has led some to conclude that Australia has not institutionalised a managerial culture in the public sector. One high-level Finance official remarked, "We have changed how the system works; we have not changed the culture of either Finance or the spending departments. The behaviour of Finance has changed more than we are often credited, but it has not been enough. We in Finance have to win the hearts and minds of our own people. That is an ongoing process; our great-grandchildren might complete the job."

But the system does work differently, and that is what matters to those who manage it. There have been great changes in rules and procedures; whether managers are more inclined to innovate than before or whether controllers still have a strong taste to impose their views on others is harder to observe. It would be naive to expect that because of the reforms, armies of managers are singularly motivated to seek out the best practice, and leave no opportunity untried in the quest for higher performance. Managers have work to do; because of the reforms they do it differently and, by most accounts, more productively. Furthermore, no one contacted for this study, and no one cited in the several government and parliamentary evaluations of the reforms, fears that the discarded rules and controls will return, or wants them to.

If reform is measured by this more realistic criterion, the picture that emerges is highly favourable. The handfuls of managers interviewed for this study and the thousands surveyed in the formal evaluations overwhelmingly agree that the public service offers more opportunity to take initiative and improve efficiency than before. A 1990 parliamentary review of FMIP concluded that is has *a*) rationalised the budget and appropriations processes; *b*) simplified the rules regulating financial management; *c*) freed up managers to use administrative resources more flexibly; *d*) enhanced the information available for accountability; and *e*) focused attention more directly on the purposes and achievements of government programmes. These findings were echoed in the government's own evaluation two years later.

Running cost arrangements

Despite these favourable conclusions, not all elements of reform have been equally successful. The government has encountered some problems in moving forward with FMIP. It is appropriate, therefore, to examine salient aspects of reform individually.

Running cost arrangements are a sensible starting point because they have been the most apparent reform to those who manage in the public service. These arrangements allow managers to spend administrative budgets (including expenditure allocated for personnel) as they see fit, with few restrictions on transferring between items. Running costs are cash limited, so that agencies must keep within agreed budgets. Moreover, minor adjustments must be accommodated within total running costs up to a threshold amount – 0.5 per cent of costs for non-recurring items, 1.0 per cent for ongoing workload changes. Adjustments above these thresholds are settled in negotiations between the spending department and Finance.

While the arrangements have contributed greatly to managerial flexibility and to fundamental changes in relations between Finance and spenders, the complicated rules give rise to tension between the departments and Finance. Although running costs comprise less than 10 per cent of total Commonwealth expenditure, they determine how much each department has to spend on its own operations. There is built-in friction in negotiating the extent to which adjustments should be allowed for workload changes or other reasons. In some conversations it appeared that managers take the flexibility provided by running costs as a powerful signal that they are to be left alone in handling this part of their budget. When Finance intrudes, they feel that it is trespassing on their responsibility. On balance, however, this tension, which is inherent in budgeting, is much less intense than in the past when Finance and departments went through hard bargaining on each spending item.

The efficiency dividend

This dividend is the most abrasive part of running cost arrangements. In budgeting for these costs, Finance adjusts the total downward by 1 per cent a year – it previously was 1.25 per cent – for expected efficiency gains. Departments see the dividend as an old-fashioned across-the-board cut; Finance sees it as a gentle means of pressuring departments to modestly improve productivity each year. A 1994 parliamentary review of the efficiency dividend, Stand and Deliver, found that it generates complaints far out of proportion to the amount saved. Some managers regard the divided "as an anomalous blunt administrative levy which is widely maligned, rarely endorsed, unsophisticated, unfair, unreasonable, and an inefficient means of saving money by cutting running costs regardless of its impact on the services delivered by government". While the parliamentary committee that conducted this inquiry found it difficult to measure actual productivity gains in the public service, it found no evidence "that the efficiency dividend has had a detrimental effect on the quality of services provided by public sector agencies". Nevertheless, to ease tensions, it recommended that the dividend be reduced to 1.0 per year, and the government accepted this recommendation.

Why has the efficiency dividend been such a sore point? In visits to headquarters and regional offices, this writer was repeatedly told of the efficiencies made possible by the new flexibility. Senior managers pointed with pride at the improved premises they have acquired by shedding staff while increasing workloads. Some of the new accommodations appear equal to those of top-rank corporations – spacious, modern and well-equipped – and paid for, as reform allows, out of the portion of the efficiency dividend retained by departments. Yet the same departments that boast of these savings gripe when a small portion is taken away. The complaints say more, it seems, about departmental attitudes toward the Department of Finance than about running costs and the dividend. Finance has been so forceful in promoting devolution from the centre of government to spending units and so committed to getting out of the way and letting managers run their own operations that just about any involvement by it in managerial matters is seen as an intrusion. On the efficiency dividend, as on other budgetary issues, newly freed up departments may still lack the maturity to appreciate Finance's continuing role in upholding the government's financial interests and its strategic responsibility for programme priorities and total expenditure.

Resource agreements

These agreements between Finance and individual departments or agencies typically provide additional resources or flexibility over a period of years. Most resource agreements pertain to running costs, but some deal with programme expenditure. Many agreements link resources provided (funding levels, additional money for acquisition of IT or other investments, retained user charges, or other resources) with actions to be taken by the department (such as cost recovery, workload increases, or upgraded information systems). Development of resource agreements has been promoted by Finance, but the process has been slowed by concern that they may reduce the government's flexibility with respect to future expenditure, as well as by a lack of guidelines and procedures. Most of those queried on the agreements regard them as a useful tool, though something that may not yet be appropriate for their own agency.

Every resource agreement is the end product of negotiations between Finance and the affected department. There is no agreement on future resources unless both sides want one and come to terms on the conditions under which resources will be made available. The several types of resource agreements in use attest to their flexibility in accommodating each agency's needs as well as the government's interest. There are five main types of resource agreements: 1) Agreements that allow agencies to retain charges levied to recover costs are now an accepted part of financial management. 2) Agreements that permit resources to vary with workload or service levels are being introduced on a limited scale. These typically have formulas that link the volume of inputs and outputs. 3) Loan agreements provide for an agency to borrow money, repayable at an agreed rate of interest, for one-time expenditures that promise future efficiency gains. 4) Agreements for the acquisition of information technology over a period of years may be financed through loans or by adjustments in the forward estimates. 5) A small number of agreements guarantee funding levels over a period of years.

Devolution

Running costs arrangements and resource agreements encourage the devolution of financial responsibility from the centre of government to spending departments. If devolution were limited to these top echelons, it would not be of much use to managers down the line who actually spend the money and deliver the services. Some Commonwealth departments are quite large and have numerous operating units and administrative layers. Government reformers have repeatedly urged that managerial responsibility be devolved throughout each department. The basic principle of devolution is that to the maximum extent appropriate, line managers should have their own budgets and the flexibility to spend within them, and they should periodically report on both the use of resources and performance. Ideally, managers should draw up annual operating plans that are consistent with the business or corporate plans prepared at higher levels.

Despite Finance's support, devolution has progressed more slowly and unevenly than it or line managers would like. Some departments have been reluctant to decentralise responsibility for fear that they will be accountable for managerial problems over which they have only weak control. In general, the larger the organisation, the more willing it has been to pass resources and responsibility down the line and the greater is its internal capacity to guide the actions of operating units. Some small departments have taken the position that giving managerial independence to field or branch offices is neither practical nor desirable.

Devolution has been slowed by a lack of expertise and training in many operating units. Devolution in haste – without an adequate managerial basis – runs the risk that lower-level managers will not be prepared to handle increased responsibility. In interviews, departmental officials recited horror stories to justify their reluctance to give managers a pot of money all their own. Several reported that each devolved unit wanted its own personnel system; a few described how every unit insisted on having its own copying machine; one complained that newly empowered managers went on a spending binge – buying equipment and adding personnel – that depleted their budgets before the year was out. Several discussed problems of assuring uniform services and quality now that every field office sets its own course.

Some of these problems are to be expected when managers are given money and authority before they acquire the know-how and the experience. These growing pains appear to be easing as more line managers learn to operate under devolution. But some kinks in devolution may outlast the start-up phase. Just as departments have had difficulty sorting out relations with central agencies – in particular the Department of Finance – so, too, have they had difficulty sorting out their relationship with devolved units. Perhaps because Australia has rejected a sharp distinction between the policymaking and service delivery functions of government, relations between top echelons and operating units tend to be fuzzy. The main exceptions encountered in this study are large departments that have a long history of standardised operations. The Department of Taxation and the Department of Social Security appear to have adapted successfully to the call for devolution. In both, regional offices have been entrusted with broad responsibility for resources, managerial initiative, and performance. These offices prepare annual work plans, they measure workload and other performance indicators, and they have been encouraged to take steps to improve operations.

Accrual accounting

FMIP has brought significant changes in financial accounting and reporting. Prior to FMIP, the Department of Finance handled the finances of all departments. This passive role for departments was inconsistent with the new doctrine of managerial responsibility. During the 1980s, therefore, the Audit Act was amended to require departments to produce their own financial statements, including a statement on assets and liabilities, in addition to the traditional cash-based reports. A further step was taken in 1992 with the requirement that depart-ments progressively move to reporting on an accrual basis. During a transitional period – extending through the 1995 financial year – departments had the option of reporting on either an accrual or modified cash basis; after then, all must report on an accrual basis. More than half of all Commonwealth departments and agen-cies moved to accrual reporting during the transition. Despite this record, the National Audit Office (NAO) has questioned whether departments are adequately prepared for the shift to accrual reporting. A 1992 NAO survey concluded that many agencies were not positioned to effectively implement previous accounting reforms and were not prepared for accrual reporting.

The previous government drew a distinction between financial reporting and budgeting. Its intention was to restrict accrual methods to financial statements; the budget would not be affected by changes in accounting principles. It would continue to be prepared and voted on a cash basis. However, as will be discussed in the concluding section to this chapter, the Commission of Audit has urged that the budget also be put on an accrual basis.

PROGRAMME MANAGEMENT AND BUDGETING

As mentioned at the outset of this chapter, PMB was launched together with FMIP in 1984. Programme budgeting (the original designation for this part of the reform package) provided a logical basis for consolidating expenditure items, but (as noted previously) the government decided not to use the programme struc-ture as the form of appropriations. As a consequence of this decision, the pro-gramme budget has been used more to provide an alternative perspective and to organise information on performance than to allocate funds. Programme Perform-ance Statements (replaced in 1994-95 by Portfolio Budget Measures Statements) and Portfolio Evaluation Plans are arrayed by programmes and subprogrammes. The programme format also has been used in Portfolio Programme Estimates, a supplementary presentation that provides background information to Parliament but is not the basis on which the budget is decided. The programme structure generated a vast amount of documentation that was hardly used by those in government or Parliament who dealt with the budget. Much of this superfluous paperwork was eliminated in the 1993-94 and 1994-95 budget cycles by recasting the budget material submitted to Parliament. The current emphasis is on information presented by portfolios. Although the portfolio-centred material is organised by programme, little would be lost if the programme structure were dropped altogether. The programme structure did, however, influence the 1987 reorganisation that created megadepartments by grouping together activities contributing to the same objective.

Despite the disappointing results of programme budgeting, the government has a useful framework for taking decisions on policies, programmes, and budgets. These decisions are centred around forward estimates, portfolio budgeting, corporate and business plans, performance information and reports, programme evaluations, and annual reports. The rules and documentation pertaining to these steps in the annual budget cycle forge a chain of events beginning with a baseline for budget decisions, moving through establishment of strategic plans and budget priorities by portfolios, the measurement of past and projected performance, the evaluation of programme outcomes, and reporting on results. To a greater degree than elsewhere, Australian budgeting pivots around reflection and retrospection on the public good to be accomplished with public money.

Forward estimates

The forward estimates are provisional decisions by the government on future expenditures. Each annual budget presents estimates for the financial year immediately ahead and forward estimates for each of the three following years. Prior to budget reform, annual deliberations on the estimates in Cabinet and Parliament focused on the next year, with the result that the outyear implications of budget decisions often were ignored. Commonwealth departments adroitly promoted programme initiatives that had low costs in the first year but ballooned to much higher outlays in the future. This behaviour led to "creeping incrementalism", with each year's budget pushed higher than the last year's by past decisions. Budget reforms in the 1980s sought to arrest this trend by having decisions on the next annual budget taken in the light of their estimated impact on future expenditures. When the government considers a programme change, the medium-term spending implications are displayed as adjustments to the forward estimates.

Although the forward estimates represent a decision by government, they do not bind future budgets. As these estimates are rolled forward each year, they are revised to reflect fresh policy changes. Yet the forward estimates are much more than multi-year projections. They are, in fact, the authoritative starting point for decisions on future budgets, the baseline against which policy changes (both savings and spending initiatives) are measured. They provisionally commit future funds to portfolios and programmes. Portfolios treat the forward estimates as entitlements to future funds; the Department of Finance sees them as the basis for budget negotiations. The forward estimates are updated from time to time to take account of government decisions, changes in economic conditions, revised estimates of participation in transfer programmes and other information affecting expenditure levels.

During formulation of the annual budget, portfolios are encouraged to finance new priorities out of savings in existing programmes. Detailed rules have been drawn up to ensure that savings are accurately calculated by departments. An increase in the forward estimates represents a policy decision that can be taken in the context of budget formulation or during any other time of the year when the government adopts measures affecting future expenditures. A proposed initiative must estimate outlays for each of the next four years. If the government accepts the proposal, the forward estimates are adjusted accordingly. Trend data show a rise in the forward estimates as they are rolled forward each year. This pattern is to be expected because the system gives departments stability with respect to future spending, while permitting them to bid for additional resources above the forward estimates. But as the forward estimates have become implanted in Commonwealth budgeting, the rate of increase has been lower than it was previously.

Officials at both the centre of government and in departments agree that the forward estimates have brought stability and discipline to the annual budget cycle. Agencies know what they are likely to have over a multi-year frame; they must estimate bids in terms of outlays over four years, and they are encouraged to seek savings in existing programmes. Budget decisions in Cabinet and its Expenditure Review Committee concentrate on the policy and spending implications of changes to the forward estimates. In a period of constrained resources, the system has eased the inevitable frictions of budgeting and has contributed to a slowdown in the growth rate of expenditure. The forward estimates were not designed to cut back expenditures or to downsize government. They were designed to harmonise programme priorities and macro-budgetary policy, and they have served this purpose well.

Portfolio budgeting

The 1987 consolidation of departments and functions into megadepartments, each headed by a minister and assisted by one or more junior ministers, strengthened the portfolios as major arenas for decisions on the budget. The consolidations had two main aims. One was to group together programmes and functions contributing to the same objective; the other was to concentrate priority-setting and resource decisions within portfolios. Portfolio budgeting gives ministers considerable discretion on establishing priorities within available resources. The arrangement generally works in the following way. Each minister is given a target for total outlays, which may include savings in existing programmes or additional spending for designated policy initiatives. The minister is then obliged to prepare a portfolio budget within the targets. Before seeking additional funds for departmental priorities, the minister is expected to look to the portfolio for offsetting savings. Even when the portfolio budget is consistent with the expenditure target, the government may impose its priorities when they differ from the minister's. Typically, however, the government will accommodate the minister's preferences, if the budget is within target. The portfolio budgeting has reduced the number of budget issues taken to the Cabinet for resolution.

Portfolio budgeting has affected the role of the Department of Finance. Pursuant to reform, its principal budget work pertains to the forward estimates rather than to the particulars of expenditure. Finance maintains the forward estimates, rebasing them as new data become available, establishing the rules and procedures for considering programme changes, monitoring budget bids to ensure that they are consistent with government policy and are supported by appropriate analysis and data, and guarding against miscalculating the expenditure impact of policy changes. Nowadays, Finance's negotiations with ministers are more likely than in the past to focus on policy issues rather than on spending details, and the analyses it prepares for the Cabinet are likely to address macro-budgeting questions.

Departmental planning

Portfolio budgeting and forward estimates have opened a channel for generating and reviewing programme changes. But it is a narrow channel, constricted by the routines and concerns of budgeting rather than by the strategic consideration of organisational objectives. In addition to having a forum for promoting and analysing policy changes, departments need to examine the implications of these changes for their own operations. The opportunity to think strategically is encouraged by corporate plans that set a department's future course and identify the concrete steps to be taken in implementing policy changes. Strategic planning is not likely to flourish – unless it is released from the routines and deadlines of budgeting. But when planning and budgeting proceed on separate tracks, there may be little inflow from one to the other. In theory, plans should drive the budget; it should set the objectives and priorities that are funded in the budget. But it does not always work out this way.

The interviews conducted for this study uncovered less interest in corporate planning than was found in the government's 1992 evaluation of the reforms. The 1992 report concluded that corporate planning has helped establish better integrated and focused departments, with shared goals and committed staff, and with a sense of the direction the organisation was headed and the steps it intended to take to get there. Some department leaders welcomed corporate planning for charting the course their newly consolidated organisation would take. Some managers reported that corporate planning was a distraction, not relevant to their work, and too time-consuming. The present study found widespread indifference to corporate planning; its utility has diminished as reform has progressed. In the early stages, when department managers were called upon to assume responsibilities that had previously been handled outside their organisation, planning was a useful means of examining the opportunities of reform. It helped make departments aware that they were indeed in charge of resources and results and that they could steer the department in a somewhat different direction than it had taken in the past. Newly empowered managers could use the planning apparatus to develop business plans for the year ahead. They could see more clearly than before how their operations fit into the larger scheme of departmental ambitions. Nowadays, by contrast, strategic planning seems to have lost much of its vitality and relevance. It is an imposed requirement, not one that ministers or managers would recurrently undertake on their own initiative. Interestingly, the down-to-earth business or operating plans continue to be useful because they specify near-term tasks and resources.

Performance information

In exchange for flexibility in using resources, ministers and managers are expected to report on the outputs and outcomes planned for the year ahead and on the results achieved in the past year. Until recently, departments submitted a vast amount of performance information to Parliament in support of their budget estimates. The volume of such information has been far greater than in any other country, but this may be a case of too much of a good thing getting in the way of effective use of the data. Prior to the 1994-95 budget, the government encouraged portfolios to publish as much information as they wanted in supplementary documents that accompanied the budget. The material added up to thousands of pages, far more than parliamentary committees could absorb in the period available for scrutiny of the estimates, and far more than was needed to communicate what was intended or had been accomplished with public funds. Beginning with the 1994-95 financial year, the volume of performance information published in connection with the budget has been greatly reduced. There is now more emphasis on systematically comparing actual against planned performance in the annual report than on detailing what will be done with the funds requested in the budget.

The government has had difficulty striking a balance between generating and publishing performance information. In the early years of reform, the official attitude seemed to be that departments would have a stronger incentive to develop performance information if the material were published. Now, however, that internal reporting systems are highly developed within departments, the government feels that it can curtail reporting requirements without risk that portfolios will disregard questions of performance in bidding for resources or in managing programmes. Furthermore, it is deemed more productive to closely examine the results actually achieved than to inundate the budget with information on what might transpire in the future.

Much of the performance data associated with the budget has been descriptive and ill focused. One could comb through the documents to find truly revealing information, but it took a lot of work to separate the merely interesting from the sharply focused and relevant information. Several characteristics of the performance information system in Australia have encouraged an abundant supply of data.

First, the Department of Finance has insisted that performance information be used for, not against, management. It should be the responsibility of individual ministers to decide how to measure and report on performance in their portfolios, provided the information satisfies government guidelines and Parliament's interest in being informed as to what departments are doing with appropriated funds. If departments want to use performance reports to depict their budget estimates in a favourable light, let them do so, as long as the information is accurate and relevant to assessing the results.

Second, encouraging departments to present information in support of their programmes has led to an arrangement in which performance indicators accompany the budget but are not tightly linked to it. Performance information is "loosely coupled" to the budget: it is available for those who want to closely examine the estimates, but there is no lockstep relationship between the resources bidden for (or provided) and the performance promised or achieved. Loose coupling has been maintained by presenting performance information in supplementary documents prepared by the various portfolios rather than in the main budget statements submitted by the government. The information stands apart from the budget but is not divorced from it.

Third, loose coupling is served by relying on performance information rather than on targets or other precise measures of results. The government is committed to improving the measurement of performance, but it is equally interested in enabling ministers and managers to provide a full report on what they have done. It prefers that ministers and managers reflect on what they have accomplished or aim to do and that they not be restricted to those dimensions that are easily quantifiable.

Finally, and most important, the government is determined that performance information extend to outcomes and not be limited to outputs. In fact, the Australian government has made a conscious effort to distinguish its broad approach to performance information from the narrower types of measures favoured in other countries. The following remarks by a senior official in the Department of Finance sets forth the Australian position on performance measurement:

> The Australian Government has taken the view that a focus on outputs alone may run the risk of allowing the focus of scrutiny to slip away from the real goals of a programme.

Programme managers could be influenced to look inward, at systems and processes, rather than assessing their actual effect on the community.

Reference to public managers in the above quote indicates that there is no demarcation between the responsibility of ministers and civil servants for performance information. In the Australian scheme of things, a manager down the line may possess valuable insights into whether a programme is performing as expected. Each manager's perspective should contribute to the flow of information on outcomes and results.

Reporting on performance has gone through three stages: 1) explanatory notes accompanying the estimates; 2) programme portfolio statements; and 3) currently, portfolio budget measure statements and annual reports. The shift from one reporting mechanism to another reflects the difficulty encountered in distilling a vast quantity of data that supports the budget and deals with broader issues of programme performance, while looking back at what was accomplished and ahead at what is planned, and encompassing both conventional output measures and more ambitious outcome information.

The Explanatory Notes (ENs) began as a means of supplementing the estimates with additional information to assist parliamentary scrutiny. One EN was prepared by each portfolio. Understandably, each portfolio saw the ENs as an opportunity to reinforce its case for the money sought from Parliament. With the advent of PMB, the ENs became vehicles for justifying the estimates in light of the results already produced or expected for the next year. By 1990, the Department of Finance characterised the ENs as the principal document by which Ministers report to Parliament and the public on the effectiveness of the programmes for which they are individually responsible. The ENs had separate outcome and outlook sections. According to the *Department of Finance Guidelines*, the latter were to provide "an assessment made in terms of progress towards or achievement of plans, targets or goals specified in the "Outlook" section of the previous year's explanatory notes"; the outlook section was to discuss "the expected effect of each variation in the appropriations on the performance of the programme element concerned". Despite – or, perhaps, because of – this structure, the ENs were extremely verbose, and parliamentary committees complained about their lack of focus. In 1988-89, the average EN for a portfolio ran about 250 pages; just two years later they averaged more than 300 pages. For the 1991-92 budget, Parliament was handed 5 418 pages of explanatory notes. The Department of Finance exercised little control over the ENs, taking the position that it was the responsibility of each portfolio to ensure the quality and relevance of the material. But given the association of these documents with the budget, portfolios were more interested in putting their best case forward than in rigorously pruning the ENs. The length of the ENs masked shortcomings in the data. The government's 1988 FMIP review found that "few indicators have been developed to a stage where they are regularly measured and those that have tend to focus on efficiency rather than effectiveness."

At the start of the 1990s, the ENs were transformed into Programme Performance Statements (PPS), but the quality of performance information was barely improved. The PPS emphasised the programme structure as a means of linking objectives, resources, and performance. However, one had to plow through an enormous amount of descriptive material to glean useful information on what was achieved with public funds. As with the ENs, each portfolio prepared its own PPS, providing a brief statement of each programme's (and subprogramme's) objectives, a description of the main elements in each programme and a much lengthier description of the activities funded in the budget, and a list of new developments anticipated in the next year. Much of the material bore directly on the portfolio's budget estimates; but, reading through the pages, it was hard to draw a conclusion on what was being spent or accomplished by each of the numerous activities inventoried in the PPS. The distinction between outputs and outcomes was muddled, and the information on future performance was quite sparse. The PPS reviewed for this report did not systematically compare performance against targets. One came away with the impression that departments had a great deal of performance information but had not yet found an effective means of communicating it.

A 1992 evaluation of public sector reforms surveyed departmental attitudes to performance information. All departments responded that they had systems for gathering performance information. Quite a few mentioned that they had or were developing an on-line capacity to access performance data. Some departments also commented on internal management practices (such as monthly or weekly meetings) to review the latest performance trends. The Department of Finance's own assessment found steady improvement in the relevance, reliability, significance, consistency and clarity of the PPS information. In their view, the improvement was due more to the programme framework for reporting on performance than to the quality of the data. The 1992 evaluation concluded that where evaluation has been carried out, performance information is of better quality. Inasmuch as the government's evaluation strategy had progressed unevenly, there was considerable variation in the quality of the performance information produced by agencies.

In 1994, the government decoupled the publication of performance information and the submission of the budget to Parliament. Most performance information now is presented in annual reports which compare the past year's financial and programme results against planned levels. As has occurred in other countries, the annual report has gained prominence as a means of holding departments and agencies accountable for their performance. Alongside this change, the Programme Performance Statements have been replaced by Portfolio Budget

Measures Statements (PBMS), which discuss the impact of programme initiatives on the budget and the forward estimates. The PBMS succinctly describes each initiative and estimates the effect on future outlays, but it provides meagre information on how the initiatives would affect outputs or outcomes. The elimination of programme information is reflected in the size of these new documents. The average PBMS is less than one-tenth the size of the comparable Programme Performance Statement. This may be a case where the government has overcorrected for the excessive documentation produced in the past. The government is confident that departments will continue to manage for performance and that an adequate supply of performance information will be available to it and Parliament on demand. One senses, however, that it will be only a matter of time before the format for reporting on performance is changed again.

Changes in reporting do not mean that the government has downgraded performance information. Of late, it has actively promoted benchmarking as a means of goading agencies to improve managerial performance. It has encouraged agencies to establish performance targets in reference to the best practices identified in comparable public or private organisations. If benchmarking spreads in the public sector, it may lead to greater emphasis on output measures that are comparable across organisations, in contrast to outcome measures that are inherently distinctive to particular programmes.

The evaluation strategy

In the Australian view, the quality of performance information depends on the quality of evaluation. If evaluation is not comprehensive and systematic, performance information will be incomplete and unreliable; it will not shed much light on whether programmes are effectively meeting policy objectives. Without a basis in evaluation, an agency may be able to gather data on service and output levels, but it is not likely to be able to measure programme outcomes. The quest for outcome data has led to an evaluation strategy that calls for systematically reviewing ongoing programmes and policy initiatives.

Although evaluation has been part of the accountability framework since the inception of FMIP/PMB, it was neglected in the early years of reform, probably because other innovations could be more readily distilled into rules and procedures. Writing in 1989, John Uhr (a leading Australian public policy expert) characterised evaluation as the most difficult component to systematise because it links organisational effectiveness and political accountability. The government may dictate that evaluations be conducted according to a preset schedule, in the same manner as budgets and annual reports are produced, but if the affected agency merely goes through the motions of fulfilling a requirement imposed by others, the material it produces will likely be stale and shallow. Genuine evaluation is more a matter of opportunity than of routine; it depends at least as much on caring about results as on sticking to the rules. Ideally, agencies would undertake evaluation when the conditions are ripe, not when a schedule calls on them to produce a report. But it is also the case that if evaluation were left to departmental initiative, many programmes would continue for years without being thoroughly reviewed. To promote evaluation, the government has sought to systematise the process while giving departments broad scope in determining how to do the job.

In 1987 the government endorsed an evaluation strategy that has gained momentum to the point where it has become one of the principal means of allocating new resources on the basis of programme effectiveness. As applied in Australia, evaluation encompasses both the retrospective assessment of programme results and the *ex ante* analysis of programme proposals. A senior official in the Department of Finance has characterised evaluation as "a state of mind. It is that constant search for relevant information on the performance of a programme which we manage and the constant search for finding options to improve that performance. The only difference between what we are referring to as evaluation and that mind-set is that we are trying to systematise that mind-set, to formalise the processes which, as professionals, we all instinctively tend to engage in."

Systematisation has proceeded through three formal requirements that have been agreed by Cabinet and have come to be known as the evaluation strategy: 1) each portfolio is required to prepare an annual portfolio evaluation plan (PEP) covering the major evaluations to be conducted over the next three years; 2) new policy proposals submitted to Cabinet must include arrangements for the evaluation to be conducted if the proposal is accepted; and 3) completed reports of evaluation are to be published, thereby permitting wide dissemination of evidence on programme performance and permitting scrutiny of the rigour and objectivity of the evaluation. The Department of Finance has invested considerable resources in promoting the evaluation strategy. It has sponsored training programmes for managers and has published a series of how-to handbooks. It periodically issues a register of completed evaluation reports, and it closely monitors the evaluation process. It has representation on many of the working groups convened to oversee particular evaluations, and it offers assistance in the conduct of individual evaluations. The Department of Finance insists, however, that the host department "owns" its evaluations and that it has the final say in how each study is conducted and who participates. The Department of Finance is mindful of departmental apprehension that evaluations will be used against them at budget time, and it has therefore been willing to take a back seat, even when the evaluation has not gone the way it wishes. But the Department of Finance has not been willing to divorce evaluations from the allocation of resources, fearing that to do so would drain them of relevance. The Department of Finance envisions evaluation as a vital responsibility of management, not as an after-the-fact-assessment by auditors. The Department of Finance officials frequently compare their approach to that taken by Canada, which established a separate office (the Comptroller General) to oversee and conduct evaluations. The Australian position is that evaluations should be conducted by those who manage the programmes, but the overall process should be guided by those responsible for allocating resources. This posture has led the Department of Finance to discourage suggestions that the National Audit Office (ANAO) review the quality of evaluations completed by departments. The Department of Finance is concerned that such audits would dampen the interest of departments in evaluating their programmes. It acknowledges that the methods and completeness of evaluations need improvement, but it is committed to improving the process by working with departments, not by taking over or second-guessing their work. The formula appears to have worked, for the Department of Finance has substantively participated in more than half of the new proposal evaluations, but always with the consent of the sponsoring department.

By requiring each portfolio to annually publish a portfolio evaluation plan (PEP), the Department of Finance hopes to transform programme review from an *ad hoc* process to one that is scheduled with as much care and forethought as are other management responsibilities. It wants the PEPs to be strategic documents that create an expectation that evaluations will be conducted on all programmes and will be completed in a timely manner, encourages ministers to participate in strategic planning for their departments, and affords the Department of Finance an opportunity to offer suggestions on portfolio evaluation priorities. With the portfolios in charge of their PEPs, these documents vary in quality and approach. Some give serious attention to the full three-year evaluation cycle, others concentrate on the year ahead and provide only sketchy information on activities beyond that year. All report on recently completed evaluations, but some take a stab at discussing how the findings affected policy, others are silent on this matter.

The Transport and Communications PEP provides standardised information on each of the more than twenty evaluations planned for the 1994-96 period: a brief description of the policy or issue to be studied, the purpose and scope of the evaluation, key issues to be addressed, the principal audience for the findings, and information on the method, resources and timing of the study. This information is briefly outlined, but the PEP conveys the impression that the portfolio has a sound basis for scheduling and carrying out its evaluations. The Social Security PEP provides a deeper description of each study to be conducted in the next year, but it only lists those to be conducted in subsequent years. Many of the dozen or so studies scheduled are to be conducted over several years, and some cover two or more programmes. This PEP specifies the issues to be explored in each evaluation, giving readers a clear understanding of the policy questions that will be addressed.

These and other PEPs have spurred a significant surge in the volume of evaluations. Between 1989 and 1993 the number of major evaluations listed in PEPs as "in progress" or "about to start" increased from 55 to 250. In addition to these major evaluations, departments file evaluation plans on some of the more routine matters scheduled for review. Although it agrees that there is room for improvement, the Department of Finance also believes that the spread of an "evaluation culture" in departments has improved the rigour and objectivity of the studies. The National Audit Office has taken a somewhat more critical view, noting that most PEPs are prepared with little involvement by ministers.

The extent to which evaluation findings are used in policy work may be a more serious concern. The Department of Finance recognises that if evaluations are not used, it will not be long before departments stop caring about them. Two overlapping channels have been established for relating evaluations to government decisions. One is the Cabinet's process for reviewing proposed policy initiatives, the other is annual work on the budget. Each submission to Cabinet advocating a course of action involving more than $5 million in annual expenditure must spell out a strategy for evaluating the initiative. According to the *Cabinet Handbook*, the evaluation strategy "should include terms of reference, key issues to be addressed, resources required for the evaluation, and timing and reporting arrangements." According to Department of Finance records, only 30 per cent of submitted proposals met this requirement in the 1992-93 budget round. Apparently many managers were reluctant to prepare detailed evaluation strategies, either because they were preoccupied with budget work or because they felt the effort would be wasted if Cabinet did not accept the policy proposal.

The budget is the second channel for influencing policy through programme evaluation. Here, too, the record has been somewhat disappointing. The proportion of spending initiatives influenced by evaluation has been highly variable: 23 per cent in 1990-91, 47 per cent the next year, but only 36 per cent in 1992-93. In fact, the success rate of policy initiatives was the same in 1992-93 for proposals influenced by evaluation as for those that proceeded independently of evaluation efforts. The weak impact of evaluations has also been found in the savings proposed by portfolios or the Department of Finance in the 1992-93 budget. Less than one quarter of the savings put forward in that budget were influenced by evaluation. These data drive home the point that evaluations are only one of a number of resources of information and influence for Cabinet. The government's policy agenda and changing political or economic circumstances may leave a deeper mark on the decisions emanating from the Cabinet.

It would be naive to expect evaluation to carry the day in the face of counter-vailing economic or political imperatives. Evaluation is likely to have the greatest impact on policy measures that are of low political salience, or when there is broad agreement on the general direction of policy but ministers have an open mind on which of several options would be most fruitful. These considerations suggest the outer limits not only of Australia's ambitious evaluation strategy but also of other management tools. Australia has tested these limits more boldly than other countries because it has not walled off policymaking from service implementation. It expects the most significant payoffs from reform to come from improved policies, not from more efficient service delivery, though it seeks that also. Aiming to reshape policy will give innovations such as the evaluation strategy a low success rate, but it may nonetheless leave a deeper imprint on government programmes and expenditures.

THE NATIONAL COMMISSION OF AUDIT

Shortly after the 1996 elections, the new government established a National Commission of Audit (NCA) to advise it on the Commonwealth's finances, including the implications of demographic changes, relations with the states and territories, and means of improving service delivery and performance. The NCA report issued in June 1996 addressed various policies and issues; the portions of the report discussed below pertain to financial management and government operations. Although it is likely that the government will adopt many of the recommendations, it is premature to assess their impact on public management. The discussion, therefore, presents relevant NCA recommendations without evaluating their actual or potential impacts.

The NCA argued that a "very substantial cultural and structural change is needed in the Australian public sector to make substantial improvements in programme delivery involving a fundamentally simplified public sector employment framework". The report hardly acknowledged any improvements resulting from the reforms introduced over the previous dozen years. Despite FMIP and PMB, it concluded that "the Commonwealth Government, like other governments, has delivered its programmes with an eye to inputs and procedures rather than to serving clients and delivering outcomes. This has led to poor programme outcomes and high costs. Programmes have become "captured" by service providers and particular interest groups rather than serving the interests of the intended beneficiaries". The report urged more widespread market-testing of services and benchmarking of performance, and it also suggested that the government's main role should be to purchase rather than provide services. "By separating and clarifying these roles, accountability is enhanced, conflicts of interest are minimised and the principles of contestability can be embedded." But the report stopped short of recommending radical changes in the structure of government. It did not call for decoupling service delivery agencies from policy departments or for budgeting and appropriating for outputs rather than inputs.

The most far-reaching proposals pertain to the Australian public service, in particular the recommendation that the career civil service be replaced by fixed-term contracts that link performance and pay and facilitate the termination of workers whose performance is unsatisfactory. The NCA also urged the government to impose a minimum efficiency target on running costs of at least 10 per cent over three years, in addition to the annual 1 per cent efficiency dividend in effect. Significantly higher savings (at least 20 per cent over three years) should be sought in organisations where reorganisation or application of information and management tools promise substantial gains.

Many of the recommendations call for improved information concerning Commonwealth performance and finances. While noting the greater prominence accorded the evaluation of programmes in Cabinet decisionmaking and budget allocations, the NCA found that the general quality of performance information was inadequate. This finding, which was supported by a 1995 assessment of performance reporting in Commonwealth annual reports, had led the Department of Finance to initiate a Performance Information Review (over a three-year period) of the objectives and performance measures of all portfolio departments.

Some of the NCA's most detailed recommendations pertained to financial information. The three main recommendations were that accrual principles be applied to the budget, that the Commonwealth should prepare government-wide financial statements, and that it should adopt a "Charter of Budget Honesty", pursuant to which the government would set and report against specific fiscal targets.

To the extent that the NCA recommendations are adopted, they are likely to elaborate the features already established under FMIP and PMB. The forward estimates system and the running costs regime would remain intact, as would the heavy reliance on formal programme evaluations and performance measures. The government would take a tougher stand in demanding efficiency and in making policy changes that contribute to its objective of eliminating the budget deficit. There would be greater use of business management practices in the public sector and less willingness to see reform as a means of enhancing the career opportunities and job satisfaction of the public service. Some of the innovations pioneered in other Commonwealth countries (especially New Zealand and the United Kingdom) would be tried in Australia.

3

FRANCE

Modernisation of the public sector has been advanced by successive governments since 1984 and is currently proceeding under principles laid down in the Rocard Circular of February 1989, a January 1990 circular concerning the establishment of responsibility centres, the 1992 Devolution Charter, and the Juppé Circular of July 1995. The most recent of these pronouncements, by Prime Minister Alain Juppé, is consistent with those issued by previous governments, both left and right of centre. But although the reforms have been repeatedly endorsed at the highest levels of government, achieving them has been a difficult, time-consuming task. Nevertheless, substantial progress has been made, devolution has advanced in a number of ministries and regions, and the pressure of budget cutbacks (including significant cuts in personnel working at the centre of government) is likely to generate additional change in the management and provision of public services.

To a greater degree than in other countries, restructuring the French public sector has a geographical dimension, for it shifts managerial control from Paris ministries to administrative offices located in regions, departments and local communities. Under the banner of devolution, the government is shifting managerial responsibility and control from central ministries to local agencies. Devolution has been spurred by efforts to make local agencies (which deliver services) more responsive to local conditions and to their customers, and to improve the performance and job satisfaction of civil servants. Modernising the public sector represents a shift from procedural rules to performance targets, from compliance with instructions handed down by superiors to negotiated decisionmaking in which service providers have an active role, from administrative fiat to partnership and participation, and from uniform rules and prescriptions to experimentation and differentiation.

Modernisation has been promoted by establishing (initially on a trial basis) responsibility centres (typically local offices providing services), which negotiate understandings with their parent ministry concerning performance yardsticks and targets, in exchange for which the responsibility centre is awarded flexibility in spending operating funds. The 1995 Juppé Circular called for this decentralised approach to be extended throughout the French public administration by the end of 1996. In addition, it provided for the pilot testing of "service contracts" in several ministries. These contracts set out service targets, the flexibility to be given service providers in negotiating and administering master budgets, including staff, methods of assessing costs and results, and the conditions under which service providers and staff would share in productivity gains. These service contracts are a logical extension of the approach pioneered with the responsibility centres.

Until recently, progress was slow and uneven because the 1989 directive authorising the establishment of responsibility centres was indicative rather than prescriptive; it encouraged a voluntary, experimental approach rather than government-wide changes in administrative practices. The pace of reform has accelerated since the adoption of the Devolution Charter in 1992, pursuant to which important innovations have been introduced in financial management and other areas of public administration. The government is now promoting a more comprehensive restructuring that will involve, it hopes, all ministries. The full impact of the 1995 change in government is not known yet, but the fact that the new regime has built on the progress made by its predecessors bodes well for the reform movement. It appears highly unlikely that the government will reverse course and recentralise management.

THE FRENCH ADMINISTRATIVE CULTURE

Compared to the other countries in this study, France still maintains a relatively centralised administrative apparatus, especially as regards personnel matters. Moreover, the probability is that, even when the current round of reforms has been completed, France will still have very large and powerful ministries at the centre of government. It also is likely to have considerable diversity in administrative practices among departments and regions.

For centuries, the hallmark of the French public administration was national rules, uniformly enforced by the central ministries in Paris. Government was run from the centre, but services were provided locally by the field offices operating in the ninety-five departments into which the country is divided. France has traditionally been very centralised in its national rules but very decentralised in its organisation. This arrangement strengthened the unity of the nation by ensuring that services were uniform throughout the country and that, regardless of where they worked, public employees saw themselves as national civil servants. Over time, the rules multiplied and administrative practices became increasingly rigid. The performance of local agencies was measured in terms of compliance with the rules, not in terms of how satisfied customers were. Formal compliance often coexisted with informal behaviour that gave lip service to the rules but tolerated deviations in practice.

Two features of traditional public administration illustrate the relationship between the centre, where control was exercised, and the regions, departments, and communities, where most national civil servants worked. One was the French civil service, which operated under detailed rules governing recruitment, job classification (there were thousands), salaries and working conditions, and other personnel matters. These rules were designed to impress upon public employees that they served the nation, not the communities in which they worked. The rules meant that a local agency in any of the departments could not hire on its own accord, but had to get approval of all salient elements of the position – the rank and salary, eligibility criteria, and even the person to be hired – from Paris. A second centralising feature was the role of a financial controller, responsible to the Ministry of Finance, in each ministry. The controller oversaw, usually *ex ante*, the expenditure of funds throughout the ministry, including spending by local agencies, to determine that they were legal and proper. Positions could not be filled, investment funds could not be committed, operating resources could not be spent without prior authorisation by the controller. Operating funds were highly itemised and reallocations required the controller's approval. Personnel and other operating expenditures were appropriated separately, and shifts between these categories were tightly controlled.

Legislation enacted during the post-war decades provided for governmental decentralisation, but despite some progress, most matters were still managed from the centre. Powerful ministries were unwilling to let go of control and local agencies were too weak to force change. However, devolution was spurred by a 1982 law that transferred certain administrative powers to local governments and agencies. For the first time, local agencies gained some leverage to push for devolution. The pressure for change was felt most strongly in the Ministry of Public Works, a vast organisation that operates in virtually every community in the country. Reforms initiated in this ministry became a model for the modernisation of the public sector.

The Ministry of Public Works was destabilised by the transfer of power to local agencies. Previously, the ministry managed construction and other projects throughout the country; it decided on the work to be done and on the resources committed to each project. The 1982 law, however, enabled local agencies to select outside contractors; they no longer had to use employees of the Public Works Ministry. To hold on to its customers, Public Works had to be responsive and competitive; it had to serve them efficiently and it had to satisfy their needs. Rather than dictating to local agencies, it had to develop a co-operative relationship that gave them some influence on how work was managed. It negotiated with local agencies concerning the work to be done, the resources to be supplied, and expected performance.

DEVOLVING MANAGERIAL CONTROL TO RESPONSIBILITY CENTRES

The Rocard Circular of 23 February 1989 (addressed by the prime minister to the Cabinet) set forth the philosophy of modernisation and established the authoritative basis for the reforms that have ensued. The circular exhorted French public administration to change because French society has changed. Noting that recent reform laws and decrees were "far from being enforced across the board", Rocard commented that "the State has never truly had the power to move beyond recommendations and exhortations. It has become evident that changes resulting from the new statutes will be brought about principally because of new personnel relations" and other improvements in the operations of government. Although Rocard did not mention the innovations under way in the Public Works Ministry, he acknowledged those public administration officials who "have played a pioneering role in this reform. I wish to encourage them and to support their efforts. Their courage and creativity must serve as a model. They should no longer feel isolated."

Rocard urged an active, participatory role for civil servants, greater sensitivity to the rights of customers, and a commitment to appraise public policies. Concerning the last of these, he declared, "There can be no autonomy without accountability, no accountability without evaluations and no evaluations without consequences". Autonomy and accountability were to be promoted through the devolution of decisionmaking to those directly concerned. Devolution means, the circular stated, "that administrative officers must be given a great deal of autonomy in decisionmaking, in operations as well as in financial matters". Toward this end, the circular called for the immediate "creation of experimental responsibility centres where more flexible financial management regulations would apply on a contractual basis, and which would be given greater administrative autonomy. The creation of a responsibility centre demonstrates the willingness of a department and the trust of administrative officials."

The establishment of responsibility centres has been a key stage in devolution. A responsibility centre is usually a departmental office of a central ministry or a local office within a department. (The term department denotes a geographical subdivision of France.) A responsibility centre is established when the parent ministry and the local office agree on performance targets and managerial flexibilities. The budget and civil service ministries also have been involved in the negotiations (typically with the parent ministry, not with the local agency) because they have to approve any special financial or personnel arrangements. Responsibility centres have been formed one at a time, as negotiations among the affected administrative organisations have culminated in agreement. Under Rocard, there was no wholesale or across-the-board authorisation of responsibility centres. But the recent Juppé Circular directs that responsibility centres be established in all ministries.

The logic of an individualised rather than blanket liberalisation of management rules was addressed in the Rocard Circular:

> For officials in charge of the centres themselves, the decision [to create a responsibility centre] implies a rigorous definition of objectives, a responsible allocation of resources, the use of modern management tools and the acceptance of outside assessments.

> Officials in charge of management and financial matters would, in turn, simply negotiate at the outset the leeway allowed each centre – an essential factor – while monitoring its performance on a regular basis.

> A contractual foundation is necessary for negotiations and control to take place. In practical terms, this means that interested agencies will have to negotiate a range of relaxations in rules applying to financial management.

Although the Rocard Circular endorsed individualised, voluntary modernisation, it directed every ministry to submit a plan indicating the measures to be taken pursuant to guidelines in the circular, including a timetable for implementing the planned measures. Moreover, Rocard told the Cabinet, "I firmly intend to see through a complete and lasting reform. It will demand both time and perseverance. I am asking you to give it the same full attention."

Further instructions on the establishment and scope of responsibility centres were specified in a follow-up circular issued by Prime Minister Rocard almost a year later, on 25 January 1990. As in the original circular, the tone was permissive – the choice of trial responsibility centres is left to the discretion of the parent government agency" – but the clear aim was to prod ministries to move more quickly in this direction. The new circular listed the types of management freedom that a ministry could grant its responsibility centres. While the terms were to be negotiated, the parent ministry had the option of providing a global authorisation of operating expenditures (excluding personnel expenditures), thereby precluding any further review by central financial controllers. Contracts between a ministry and its responsibility centres would normally be for three years, and they would arrange for the ministry to periodically (annually or semi-annually) monitor the centre's performance. Each year, the ministry and each of its responsibility centres would jointly assess results by reference to the objectives set in the contract. Near the end of the contract period, the two organisations would undertake a comprehensive assessment of the centre's operations for the whole contract period, following which a decision would be taken on continuing or modifying the arrangement.

The approach taken in the two circulars was cautious and tentative. No change was made in the legal status of local agencies; instead, ministries had the option of providing global authorisation of operating expenditures, excluding personnel costs, in lieu of the specific authorisations provided prior to devolution. Flexibility was to be provided within a framework of national rules and was to be provided on a case-by-case basis, and then only for three years at a time. As allowed by the circulars, some ministries moved quickly and comprehensively, while other dragged their feet and established few or no centres. The Ministry of Public Works, which initiated its own modernisation four years before the first Rocard Circular, accounted for most of the early progress. In 1992, nearly 80 per cent of civil servants working in responsibility centres were employed in this ministry. Progress also was uneven in devising "service projects" – strategic plans that defined the objectives of the responsibility centres, the changes to be introduced to improve customer services and other measures of performance, and how resources would be used. The Rocard circulars made the formulation of a service project a precondition for setting up a responsibility centre. But some centres were established without any advance strategic planning, and others gave only perfunctory attention to this requirement. Some, however, used the service project as an opportunity to undertake a strategic assessment of their goals and operations.

BROADENING THE REFORMS

In the past several years, a number of steps have been taken to extend devolution and modernisation throughout the national administration. One has been a shift from viewing the responsibility centres as experiments to treating them as the expected and legitimate arrangements; another has been adoption of the Devolution Charter; the third has been the introduction of standard methods for modernising and devolving managerial control; and the fourth has been the Juppé pronouncement that mandated universal implementation. As responsibility centres have become the norm, their number has grown from fewer than 100 in 1992 to more than 200 the next year and to about 350 in early 1995. Government officials expect almost 700 centres to be in operation when the reform is fully implemented.

The 1992 Devolution Charter and the decrees issued pursuant to it have sought to define the managerial scope of the various levels of public administration. Article I of the charter declares:

Devolution is the general rule for the allocation of responsibilities and resources among the various hierarchical levels of the government's civil administration.

The primary responsibilities of the ministries and other central organs of government are to establish goals for devolved agencies, evaluate their needs and allocate resources, and assess results. Regional authorities manage investment funds and also co-ordinate activities involving multiple departments in the region. Local agencies in the departments implement regional and community programmes and spend the operating funds allocated to them by central administration. This division of responsibility has some resemblance to the separation of policymaking from programme implementation and service delivery that has been institutionalised in other countries. Under the Devolution Charter, central ministries are to withdraw from operational matters; they should concentrate instead on strategic issues. To spur this role shift, the government has begun to reduce staffing in ministries by replacing only half of those who retire.

The Devolution Charter is a legal blueprint for parcelling out functions among the levels of government. It unites the two main themes of modernisation: improving services to citizens and customers and improving the internal performance of ministries. Those promoting reform recognise that change has been more eagerly embraced in the field than in the centre. To stimulate change, the Devolution Charter assigned responsibility for progress to the Interdepartmental Committee on Regional Administration. This committee has monitored compliance with devolution policy and has published an annual progress report. In addition, each ministry prepares an annual report specifying the powers and duties devolved during the previous year and those scheduled for devolution in the next year.

Function-by-function devolution depends on the judgement of the parent ministry as to whether it or local agencies should be in charge. An official assessment argued that progress was slow because it depended on the willingness of ministries to transfer functions to lower echelons. It insisted that devolution not be limited to the simple desire to delegate the performance of State activities to the most appropriate devolved agency. Just as important is the need to create zones of autonomy around devolved agencies within which they will be able to discuss and steer implementation of public policies. It called for face-to-face dialogue between central government and local agencies on what their respective roles should be. In other words, local agencies should be full partners in the devolution process. The report recommended that each agency have a devolution committee, comprised of central and local officials, that would suggest the functions to be assigned to each level.

FINANCIAL MANAGEMENT

In recent years, the budget ministry has actively promoted the modernisation of financial management. There has been a marked trend toward consolidation of operating expenditure (excluding personnel). Since 1991, ministries have been encouraged to group funding for equipment and supplies, premises, the purchase

of vehicles, travel expenses and services in a single budget chapter. As a consequence, the number of separate chapters for these expenditures declined from
1 472 in 1984 to 903 a decade later, and further consolidation is under way.
Moreover, the budget ministry has requested ministries to make consolidated
allocations to devolved agencies. The budget ministry also has broadened procedures for reallocating funds during the year, including redistributions between
departments, and allowing local agencies to retain certain operating revenues.
Unused operating funds may be selectively carried over to the next year, but
there are legal barriers to the general carryover of these funds. However, the
government has liberalised the precommitment of the following year's funds,
permitting an amount equal to one quarter of current year's operating funds to be
committed during the last two months of the financial year. In fact, ministries may
transfer funds in advance to devolved agencies, thereby making money available
to them at the very start of the new fiscal year.

Financial control is being reorganised to shift from financial controllers
located in each ministry to controllers placed in each department. The system has
been tested in two regions, and full implementation has been endorsed by the
Juppé Circular discussed in the next section. The principal idea is that rather than
controlling everything from the centre – with the same rules applied in all regions
and departments – local variation is permitted. Presumably, the departmental
financial controller will be more responsive to local conditions than would one
stationed in Paris.

The government also has adapted the degree of financial control to the
managerial competence and performance of each agency. The new financial control system shifts from controlling specific expenditures to controlling the financial
procedures maintained by each department. A four-scale rating system has been
introduced, keyed to an assessment of each agency's internal controls:

Rating	Form of financial control
No serious deficiencies.	A global budget, no allocation to specific expenditure items, except for certain personnel expenses.
Some serious irregularities, but not wide-spread.	Allocations controlled by category of expenditure.
More widespread irregularities.	Specific authorisation for certain expenditures.
Generalised deficiencies in internal controls.	Specific authorisation required for all expenditures.

The assessment on which the above rating is based covers the local draft budget prepared by the agency, the management report, the budget control system, observations by the accountant and methods of control.

To encourage the devolution and modernisation of financial management, a standard contract between the budget ministry, the civil service ministry and the parent ministry has been developed for establishing responsibility centres. It no longer is necessary to negotiate with the central ministries over each term of the contract. However, the local agency must still negotiate with its parent ministry concerning the resources and performance of the responsibility centre.

Early assessments of the responsibility centres (in 1991 and 1992) found consensus that management had been improved, the quality of services to users had been enhanced, managers had greater flexibility in using resources and had greater awareness of costs, and that the process of decentralisation had been strengthened. Most centres had a more participatory style of management than before and gave attention to objectives and performance. But the studies also found that progress was slow and uneven, relationships with the central administration still strained, and management of the workforce still highly inflexible. Attitudes toward the modernisation process also were tainted by recurring budget crises and efforts to reduce the size of the public service. In France, as elsewhere, the promise of medium-term financial stability faded in the face of pressure to cut public expenditure. Responsibility centres that had expected to use efficiency savings to improve the working environment or services to users found that they had to make do with less.

THE JUPPÉ CIRCULAR

Shortly after becoming prime minister, Alain Juppé issued a circular that once again called for modernising the public service. It identified five priority objectives that were similar to those pursued by his predecessors: 1) the functions of the state and the provision of public services should be clarified; 2) government should be more responsive to the needs and expectations of the public; 3) central government should be reformed; 4) responsibilities should be delegated to operating units; and 5) public management should be overhauled. The fact that similar objectives have been articulated by previous governments indicates that while the goals of modernisation are widely shared, achieving them across the full spectrum of the public administration is very difficult.

The Juppé Circular announced a number of initiatives that built on previous developments. These included: a citizens and public services charter that, in addition to upholding traditional principles (such as neutrality and equality), would emphasise quality, accessibility, simplicity, speed, transparency and other values; quantitative and qualitative targets to improve public services; the systematic decentralisation of services, accompanied by significant reductions (10 per cent in the first year) in the staffing levels of the central administration; the reorganisation of regional and local services; and the reorganisation of relations between the central government and service providers.

Two features of the Juppé Circular warrant particular mention. First, the circular embraced the principle that the policy role of the modern state (to anticipate, analyse, plan, legislate and evaluate) should "be clearly distinguished from the administrative role, which is to manage, enforce regulations or deliver services. There is no need for this latter role to be centralised". This separation of policy from operations would be promoted by downsizing central ministries and decentralising managerial responsibilities. Second, the circular directed all ministries to extend the responsibility centre concept throughout the public administration. The circular called for responsibility centres to be universally implemented by the end of 1996. In addition, performance contracts are to be pilot-tested in several ministries.

Although the French modernisation campaign was begun a decade ago, it is not yet at a point where the reforms can be evaluated as fully as in other countries. Some ministries have taken up modernisation only recently, and it will be a number of years before the Juppé initiatives are incorporated into public administration. Although the principles of devolution and modernisation have been accepted by every recent government, progress has been slowed by the centralised culture of public administration. Reshaping this culture will be a difficult challenge for modernisation of the public service.

4

NEW ZEALAND

The New Zealand public sector is managed very differently today than it was in the late 1980s, when the government launched what many regard as the most comprehensive and far-reaching reform in the OECD community. These reforms were initiated by two laws – the State Sector Act 1988 and the Public Finance Act 1989 – that were conceived as a package and have been characterised by the New Zealand Controller and Auditor General as "enormous, ambitious, and in large part unprecedented anywhere in the world". Legislative requirements have been supplemented by a series of managerial innovations, including purchase and performance agreements, strategic result and key result measures, departmental forecast reports, strategic plans, and a variety of accountability instruments. These and other innovations compose what Jonathan Boston and his associates have labelled the New Zealand Model, "a carefully crafted, integrated, and mutually reinforcing reform agenda". The model's "conceptual rigour and intellectual coherence" distinguish it from the management reforms adopted in other countries.

To a far greater degree than any other country, New Zealand has sought to structure public management along the lines of business organisations operating in a market economy. It has not privatised core government responsibilities – with the exception of State-owned enterprises, government activities still are in public hands, though there has been greater reliance on contracting out. Instead, the government has adapted market-type mechanisms to the management of public organisations. For example, government budgets and financial statements are on an accrual basis; appropriations are voted for on the basis of outputs rather than inputs; departments pay a capital charge on their net assets and manage their own bank accounts, paying or earning interest depending on the size of their cash balance; each department is headed by a chief executive who is appointed for a fixed term and has freedom to employ senior managers, spend appropriated funds, and take other managerial actions as she or he deems suitable; chief executives negotiate annual agreements specifying their performance and that of their departments; and financial results and outputs are periodically compared to planned levels.

In line with the adoption of business practices, the New Zealand model distinguishes between the government's interest as a purchaser of departmental outputs and its interest as the owner of the entity. As purchaser, the government is interested in getting the best price for the services it acquires; as owner, it is interested in the financial soundness of the entity and its long-term capacity to perform. Its purchase interest is expressed in annual contract-like agreements that specify the outputs to be supplied by the department and the amount to be paid by the relevant minister; its ownership interest is expressed in audited financial statements and in other assessments of departmental capacity.

Before reform, New Zealand had a centrally controlled state sector. Departments had little discretion in managing their resources or in carrying out assigned tasks. They were expected to comply with *ex ante* rules, and they generally were not held accountable for how well they performed. All departments were constrained by detailed civil service rules and other centrally prescribed and enforced regulations. "One-size-fits-all" management was practised by the Treasury, which issued voluminous guidelines covering just about every type of administrative action involving the expenditure of public funds; by the State Services Commission, which regulated the employment of civil servants and set their salaries and working conditions; and by an agency that decided where department offices were located and how much rent they paid. Each department had a permanent head who served indefinitely, regardless of the organisation's performance or the cognisant minister's preference.

This command-and-control regime reached to the private sector as well. Prior to reform, New Zealand had one of the most regulated and subsidised economies among OECD Member countries. Market competition was dulled by currency and trade controls and by myriad regulations that sheltered domestic industries from foreign competition and often from new domestic entrants into their markets as well. The government owned and managed major enterprises, especially in the transport and communications sectors. State enterprises were operated as if they were departments, with the government setting prices and wages. At times, official unemployment levels were kept artificially low by staffing state enterprises with persons who might otherwise have been out of work.

During the post-war era, these inefficiencies were veiled by a robust economy and an expansive welfare state. Prior to the first oil shock in 1973-75, New Zealand had one of the highest growth rates in the OECD community, as well as some of the most comprehensive and generous welfare programs. Unemployment was low and prices were stable, and New Zealand's economy was buffered against international disturbances by preferential trade relations with the United Kingdom, which imported most of what the country wanted to sell. This protected condition was abruptly ended, however, by world-wide stagnation in the 1970s and by the United Kingdom's entrance into the Common Market. The former spawned high inflation and high unemployment, while the latter deprived New Zealand of its secure overseas market. During the 1975-84 period, New Zealand's economic performance deteriorated, leaving the country with one of the lowest growth rates among OECD Member countries. The government responded to the economic crisis by tightening controls, increasing subsidies, and investing in megaprojects that would, it hoped, give New Zealand self sufficiency in energy resources. These ventures misfired, and by 1984 economic conditions no longer were sustainable and the country faced a run on its currency. As confidence dropped, consensus emerged that strong measures were needed to reverse the decline. Following a mid-year election, the new Labour government embarked on a series of reforms that unfolded in three stages through the remainder of the decade. The first stage (commencing shortly after the election) deregulated the economy, the second (two years later) sought to put state-owned enterprises on a business-like basis, and the third (initiated in 1988) restructured public management. The perceived successes of economic deregulation and the reform of state enterprises paved the way for rapid and comprehensive reform of the public sector.

New Zealand is unique among the countries discussed in this report, for it alone revamped public management through legislation rather than by administrative action. It was able to legislate speedily and decisively because the country had a one-chamber Parliament and a one-party government. New Zealand's small size and unitary structure also encouraged reform via legislation, as did the close working relationship between ministers and senior Treasury officials and the availability of a body of ideas (sometimes referred to as the new institutional economics or new public management) that gave ministers and officials confidence to innovate without first pilot-testing the reform.

The State Sector Act 1988 replaced permanent department heads with chief executives who serve for renewable terms of up to five years under employment contracts negotiated between them and the State Services Commissioner. These contracts have standard terms – pay, working conditions, provisions for removal from office, and so on. More substantive provisions keyed to each chief executive's departmental responsibilities are negotiated in an annual performance agreement between the chief executive and the Responsible Minister. These agreements set out the specific criteria used in assessing the chief executive's performance. They typically focus on the priorities to be pursued by the chief executive, and they establish targets and milestones for achieving particular results. The performance agreements emphasise that the chief executive is accountable for the department's performance. The State Sector Act gives chief executives full managerial responsibility for their departments, including authority (delegated to them by the State Services Commissioner) to hire and compensate staff and negotiate collective agreements. Subsequent legislation (the

Employment Contracts Act 1991) placed private and public employment on the same basis. It accords all employees the option of working under individual or collective contracts.

The managerial role of chief executives was further enhanced by the Public Finance Act 1989 (PFA). This act provides for appropriations to be made by output classes rather than by inputs, and for both the budget and appropriations to be on an accrual basis. The change in the basis of appropriations gave chief executives broad discretion to select the mix of inputs to be used in generating outputs. The 1989 law sought to advance the measurement of performance by distinguishing between outputs (the goods and services produced by departments) and outcomes (the results or impacts of government outputs on society). Outcomes are the responsibility of ministers, while outputs are the responsibility of chief executives. PFA provides for the *ex ante* specifications of outputs; it conceives of the budget and ensuing appropriations as "contracts for performance" which specify the resources allocated for the supply of outputs.

Although the budget has more than 300 departmental output classes, plus another 150 non-departmental output classes and almost 300 other types of appropriations, these are too few to establish the basis on which performance is measured and monitored. Some output classes exceed one billion dollars, a large amount for a country the size of New Zealand. To obtain more specific output targets, the government has prescribed that annual purchase agreements be negotiated between Ministers and chief executives. These agreements detail the activities the department plans to carry out with the resources provided to it. Each department periodically compares actual versus planned financial results and outputs.

These arrangements are predicated on a sharp distinction between the roles of ministers and chief executives. The former are purchasers of services, the latter are providers. As purchaser, the Minister has the option of obtaining services from either public or private suppliers, though, in fact, most outputs are produced by departments and Crown entities. These public entities are owned by the government, but they operate outside the departmental structure. The budget describes (in detail, for some departments; only sketchily for others) the government's planned outcomes, but it does not explicitly allocate resources on this basis, nor does it hold chief executives accountable for achieving them. As mentioned earlier, these executives are accountable only for the outputs produced by their departments.

Linking outputs and resources requires a further distinction, already noted, between the government's interest as purchaser of outputs and its interest as owner of departments. As purchaser, the government makes appropriations to acquire a certain volume of outputs; as owner, it makes appropriations to provide the entity with capital. PFA provides for several types of appropriations that correspond to this distinction. In addition to appropriations by output classes, appropriations are made for capital contributions as well as for grants and benefit payments, for which no output is provided in return. PFA recognises that some outputs purchased by the government are contestable, while others are supplied only by a public entity. When outputs are contestable, PFA authorises a department to budget its trading revenue on a net basis; it may spend all such revenue. Other output classes, however, are appropriated on a gross basis. In fact, contestability is not as widespread as was envisioned when PFA was drafted, and all but a few output classes have gross appropriations. PFA also anticipated that over time many appropriations would be based on output prices rather than on input costs. The former are defined by PFA as Mode C appropriations for acquiring a specified class of outputs required by the Crown; the latter as Mode B appropriations for the costs to be incurred in the supply of a specified class of outputs. Almost a decade after PFA was enacted, most appropriations remain on a Mode B basis because cost accounting and allocation systems are not yet sufficiently developed to permit appropriations on the basis of price.

Despite the comprehensive and creative arrangements prescribed by the State Sector and Public Finance Acts, it is important to note that public sector innovations have continued to be made in the 1990s. Part of the reason is that legislation inherently is incomplete; it must be defined and implemented through administrative actions. Another reason for ongoing innovation is that, as the reforms were implemented, the government and senior managers became aware of gaps and shortcomings in the original design. Innovations have been made to enhance the government's capacity to define its strategic objectives and means of enforcing accountability. The recent innovations have been congruent with the original reforms, though some have moved in directions that might not have been foreseen when the State Sector and Public Finance acts were developed. Additional refinements are likely to be introduced in the years ahead, but if the basic design is retained, they will be more modest than those that have been made thus far.

The innovations indicate that evaluation of the reforms has been ongoing. During the 1990s, numerous task forces and interdepartmental groups have examined one or another facet of the New Zealand model. Often the changes proposed by these groups have been implemented by the government. The net effect has been increased formalisation of public management. Whereas the original legislation left many administrative details to be filled in by managers, managers at present are required to comply with numerous government-wide standards and procedures. In fact, most of the currently required plans and reports were added after the initial legislation was enacted. There is some concern that a new compliance regime is seeping into New Zealand management. In contrast to the old regime, which demanded compliance with *ex ante* input controls, the new regime demands compliance with rules for specifying and documenting perform-ance. Although each performance specification or reporting requirement may be justified, the cumulative burden unwittingly diminishes risk-taking initiatives by New Zealand managers.

This and other facets of the New Zealand model will be examined in the remaining sections of this chapter. But before evaluating the various components of the system, it would be appropriate to assess the overall results. The first comprehensive assessment of the reforms was made in 1991 when the incoming National government faced a decision as to whether it should retain the innova-tions adopted by the Labour government that had preceded it. This assessment, generally referred to as the Logan Review, strongly endorsed the reforms, though it also offered a number of recommendations to ameliorate some problems that had emerged during the initial implementation. The Logan Review found that in the first few years they had been in effect, the reforms had a beneficial impact on the efficiency and effectiveness of the public service. Senior managers reported that they had increased freedom to manage, along with increased accountability for results. They also confirmed that performance had improved in many key areas. On the negative side, the Logan Review expressed concern that the collec-tive interest had been weakened and that there was some confusion and tension in the relationship between ministers and chief executives. But the Logan Review emphatically urged that the reforms be retained, and the new government unequivocally adopted this recommendation.

Several assessments of the New Zealand model were published during 1996. All concluded that the reforms have made a positive contribution to public management, but each found some shortcomings. The 1996 OECD *Economic Survey of New Zealand* characterised the reforms "as a remarkably coherent attempt to address some fundamental problems traditionally afflicting public sector govern-ance. These reforms have brought about a marked reduction in the scope of the government's activities and in its size relative to the rest of the economy". But the Survey concluded that although considerable progress had been made, the gov-ernment could still do more to pressure and enable its agencies to improve their performance:

> For instance, there is scope to make the supply of services it buys truly contestable. To enhance its own ability to learn and innovate, the government could put in place better systems for evaluating policies empirically. Moreover, it is questionable whether the reliance on the contractual framework alone is sufficient, in particular where outputs are dicult to measure.

First, there is a significant difference between the extent to which the New Zealand model preaches and practices contestability. Most public services are purchased from core departments or Crown entities, not from outside suppliers. Although appropriations are voted to ministers, most funds are actually spent by departments or other public agencies. Second, there has been under-investment in formal programme evaluation, and less-than-anticipated attention to outcomes. Finally, contract-like instruments such as purchase and performance agreements do not create genuine arms-length relationships between Ministers and managers. If, as new institutional economists argue, ministers were "captured" by service providers before reform, they may not be able to escape capture afterwards.

Another assessment was prepared by this author in a 1996 report titled *The Spirit of Reform: Managing the New Zealand State Sector in a Time of Change*. Sponsored by the State Services Commission and the Treasury, this report found that:

> Both within government and among outside observers ... there is overwhelming consensus on the superiority of the reformed system and hardly any sentiment for dismantling the new arrangements and going back to centralised control; the reforms have improved the efficiency and quality of public services by encouraging managerial initiative and rewarding success. Managers have a much clearer understanding of their role and responsibilities; more timely and complete data on the cost of doing business and on what they are accomplishing with public funds; greater awareness of the needs and interests of clients and customers; and expanded opportunity to change operating procedures, the use of resources, and working conditions.

This study, which was drawn largely from interviews with ministers and managers, found an undertone of complaints about the new system, as the following quotation from the report indicates:

> Some managers complain about the sinking lid on operating budgets, with no adjustment for inflation and across the board cuts. Some... complain about having to work harder in a more competitive and less stable environment and without sufficient resources to accomplish all that is expected of them. They feel that the government is indifferent to rising workloads and that doing more is not compensated in the budget. One widely heard complaint is that despite cost and performance data, budget levels still are set arbitrarily, without genuine analysis of what it takes to complete assigned tasks. Quite a few ocials, especially those in small departments, commented on the burden of complying with burgeoning information and reporting demands of central agencies and Parliamentary committees.

In judging the import of these and other complaints, one must be mindful that the interviews were structured to identify problems and issues, not to assess the New Zealand model. Inevitably, therefore, negative comments outweighed positive ones. But the most telling conclusion, almost universally shared, is that the new system is far superior to the old one. This view is held as firmly by those who have voiced complaints as by those who find little or no fault.

The assessment of New Zealand reforms offered in this chapter also concentrates on perceived problems or shortcomings. Many of the complaints, however, have been generated by the elevated standards and expectations promoted by the reforms. For example, once New Zealand had few output measures; now managers question whether the measures are properly specified, whether they are sufficiently linked to budget and appropriations decisions, and whether the art of performance specification can be more fully extended to outcomes. Once there were no performance or purchase agreements; now managers wonder whether the terms are clearly specified and strictly enforced. Once capital supplied by the government to its departments was free; now managers argue whether the capital charge has been properly calculated. Elevated expectations have generated considerable griping, but they also are a measure of the progress that has been made in raising the standards of public management.

STRUCTURING GOVERNMENT DEPARTMENTS AND AGENCIES

The structure of public organisations is a useful starting point for detailing and assessing the New Zealand reforms. It is an article of faith in the new public management that organisations that have multiple, conflicting objectives, such as those which commingle policy advice and service delivery, are inherently inefficient. The 1987 brief, *Government Management*, argued that when policy and operations are merged in the same organisation, those who make policy are vulnerable to capture by those who provide the services. It urged, therefore, that service delivery be decoupled from policy advice. Placing the two responsibilities in separate entities would enable Ministers to obtain advice that was not biased by the interests of service providers. Yet the brief also suggested that organisational structure be decided "on a case-by-case basis in the light of resource constraints and current priorities." In practice, the reorganisation of departments has eschewed doctrinaire solutions. Some departments continue to be integrated; they combine both policy and operational responsibilities; others have been decoupled and are responsible only for advising the government and monitoring the performance of service providers. For example, early in the reform era, the Ministry of Transport was divested of roads, highway safety, airports, and other services; as a consequence, it is now a small department with fewer than 100 staff members, compared to the approximately 8 000 it employed before reorganisation. On the other hand, the Department of Social Welfare (whose current chief executive previously headed the Department of Transport) remains a very large organisation with responsibility for an array of social programmes.

The logic of reorganisation in New Zealand is substantially different from that which led to the establishment of Next Step agencies in the United Kingdom. These agencies were created to give them operating independence from Whitehall – the centre of British government. New Zealand agencies have been created to free the core departments from capture or undue influence by subordinate units. The concern that policy makers will be captured by service providers induced the establishment of New Zealand Defence Forces as a separate operating unit from the Ministry of Defence. The Ministry is responsible for policy;

Defence Forces has operational responsibility. There is widespread recognition that this reorganisation was flawed, and the two entities have found it necessary to develop means of co-ordinating policy work and defence operations.

Unlike the defence reorganisation, which was driven by cutting-edge management theory, most of the decoupled departments have been restructured on more pragmatic grounds. The Department of Justice, which was reorganised in 1995, is an interesting case in point. Before it was decoupled, the Department was a sprawling organisation whose operational responsibilities included the courts and special tribunals, prisons and other correctional institutions, and the public registry of death, births, land transfers, and other significant events. The Department also had a policy role concerning law reform and the criminal justice system. A review of the Department performance found that policy responsibilities and certain operational functions had been neglected. The solution was to divest the various operational tasks (which had little connection to one another) and to recast the Department of Justice into a policymaking unit. Reorganisation of this Department indicates that the form of organisation may depend on the affinity of operating units. When the work of these units supports common objectives, there may be considerable value in housing them in the same department. In these cases, the preferred solution may be to retain an integrated department, even though it merges policy and operations. When, however, operating units have little to do with one another (as was the situation in the Department of Justice), decoupling is likely to be the favoured course of action.

However, even when conglomerate departments remain intact, the preferred practice has been to restructure their components (including the policy unit) into separate business units, each with its own objectives, performance targets, business manager, and operating budget. This structure may enable the department to separate policy from operations while facilitating co-ordination among the various units. The Social Welfare and Labour Departments have both evolved in this manner.

When a department is decoupled, the separated units often become Crown entities, a catchall category that includes all government entities that are not core departments or State-owned enterprises. (In some cases, the newly separated units become core departments, as happened when the Department of Correction was established as part of the reorganisation of the Department of Justice.) As a residual category, Crown entities come in various forms and cover a wide range of responsibilities. Many of these entities have operational responsibilities, others are regulatory agencies, and a few have a policy role. Through amendments to the Public Finance Act and other actions, the government has placed Crown entities on approximately the same footing as the core departments. Each Crown entity is required to prepare an annual statement of intent specifying its objectives, activities and performance targets, as well as an annual report (including audited financial statements) comparing actual performance against the targets set out in its statement of intent. Moreover, most Crown entities enter into funding agreements that are similar to the purchase agreements negotiated by the departments. Despite these formal requirements, there often is less transparency in the financing and operations of Crown entities than in those of departments, as well as weaker accountability. Although the Public Finance Act gives ministers considerable power to guide the Crown entities, these units typically are controlled by boards who appoint the chief executives, in contrast to departments whose chief executives are directly appointed by the government. Moreover, there sometimes is an elongated chain of accountability that weakens the government's capacity to dictate, or be adequately informed of, how Crown entities are operated. The problem is especially evident in the health sector, where the Ministry of Health (a policy unit) negotiates funding agreements with four Regional Health Authorities (purchasing units), which contract for health services from 23 Crown Health Enterprises (service providers), which in turn obtain services from various local providers. When the management chain is as elongated as this one, it may be difficult for the government to get the outputs it wants. For example, when the government allocated additional funds to mental health care, it sometimes found that the money went for other services, not the ones it thought it was purchasing. In these and similar cases, the government holds both the political and financial risks, but it may nevertheless lack sufficient leverage to obtain the results it wants. Since Crown entities carry out some of the most vital and expensive public services, there is growing pressure to reconsider their status and relationship to ministers and departments. Law and practice have evolved rapidly in the 1990s, and further developments are likely in the years ahead. But because of the enormous variety in Crown entities, it may be difficult to devise rules that cover all.

Each Crown entity is under the responsibility of a minister who relies on the cognisant department for policy advice and other assistance. Because some decoupled departments are very small, they may lack sufficient staff and the appropriate mix of skills to contract with and monitor the performance of Crown entities. Quite a few departments are weaker than the Crown entities within their purview. It is a mistake to regard decoupled departments solely as policy organisations. Advising ministers typically is only one of their responsibilities, but not always the most important or demanding one. These departments do not always have the necessary resources to effectively maintain accountability within the public sector.

The unbalanced relationship between some (not all) Crown entities and the government has been aggravated by New Zealand's preference for a large number of small departments. The government is organised into almost 40 departments, a far greater number than in most OECD Member countries. Most departments have small staffs to carry out policy, monitoring, and reporting duties. The last of these may be particularly burdensome, and some departments are under-resourced to fulfil all their managerial responsibilities. Moreover, the large number of small departments, the proliferation of Crown entities, and other organisational changes have stirred concern that the collective interest has been weakened by the reforms. The 1991 Logan Review gave careful consideration to this matter. Since then, interdepartmental policymaking and co-ordination have been broadened and strengthened by the development of strategic result areas that define government-wide priorities and by the requirement that each department set out its key result areas that are congruent with the government's strategic objectives. These innovations have been successfully institutionalised; they have lessened concern that departmental perspectives are too narrow and that policies are not sufficiently integrated. Other conditions that have fostered the collective interest are New Zealand's small size, its strong public ethic, and the relative ease of communicating across departments.

MINISTERS AND MANAGERS

Every department is the responsibility of a minister and is headed by a chief executive. As noted in the introductory section of this chapter, New Zealand distinguishes between the role of ministers as the purchasers of outputs and of managers as the suppliers of the outputs. This division of responsibility is reflected in the form of the budget and appropriations. Appropriations are voted to ministers who have discretion to acquire outputs from whatever source they prefer. In most cases, departments are the suppliers, except in those sectors where the bulk of outputs are provided by Crown entities. Some departments supply outputs to two or more ministers, each of whom has a purchase relationship with it. In these cases, the minister with the greatest stake in the department's performance is designated the Responsible Minister.

The Responsible Minister looks after the government's ownership interest, including the department's financial condition and its capacity to perform. However, the Responsible Minister is not the employer of the department's chief executive. Chief executives are appointed by the State Services Commissioner pursuant to elaborate search and (in the case of reappointment) evaluation procedures. The Responsible Minister does negotiate an annual performance agreement with the chief executives. There is thus a triangular relationship between Ministers, chief executives and the State Services Commission. Some have suggested that the relationship be simplified by removing the Commissioner's role as the employing authority; others argue, however, that the Commissioner provides a broader perspective than would be likely if the minister and chief executive had bilateral contracts.

It is widely accepted that although management performance may generate considerable political risk, ministers should not participate in the day-to-day operations of departments. In the New Zealand model, their responsibility reaches to policy guidance, providing resources, monitoring performance and enforcing accountability. Nevertheless, the dual roles of ministers and chief executives may make it difficult to determine where one's accountability ends and the other's begins. The conceptual distinctions drawn by the New Zealand model sometimes breaks down in practice. By design, the minister is accountable to Parliament and the chief executive is accountable to the minister; the minister is responsible for policy, the chief executive for operations; the minister is responsible for outcomes, the chief executive for outputs. These distinctions may not be sufficiently determinative when there are actual or perceived shortcomings in departmental performance. Probably the most publicised such shortcoming was the collapse of a platform built by employees of the Department of Conservation that resulted in the deaths of more than a dozen hikers. In the aftermath of this tragedy, the responsible manager initially refused to resign, claiming that the operational failure was the responsibility of the chief executive. The latter also refused to resign, claiming that the failure was the responsibility of those who designed and built the platform.

Fuzziness is inherent in a relationship that assigns political risk to the minister and managerial discretion to the chief executive. It may take considerable time for the division of responsibility to be clarified, for as long as both the minister and the chief executive have a say in what the department performs, both or neither may be called to account. The New Zealand model presumes that ministers will be tough bargainers, striving to get the best deal for the government, as well as demanding evaluators who insist that chief executive and departmental performance meet expectations. But these roles see the chief executive principally in the role of purchaser rather than as owner of the entity. The two roles pull responsible ministers in opposite directions. As purchaser, a minister should maintain an arms-length relationship with the department; as owner, by contrast, a minister must take a proprietary interest in the department. In this clash of interests, ownership almost always has come in second best, for it is a weaker, less compelling influence than that which a minister has in allocating resources and contracting for the next year's output.

The government has recognised that greater priority should be accorded to ownership, but it has not yet found an effective means of reorienting ministers in this direction. Annual performance agreements now have a standard annex that incorporates the government's "collective ownership interest", but this provision does not have the same stature or detail as the purchase agreement. More to the point, as purchasers, ministers have incentives to behave in ways that weaken the ownership interest. When they exert downward pressure on departmental operating budgets, ministers may unwittingly take away essential resources (for training and equipment, for example) needed to ensure future performance. There is reason to believe that small departments have been especially hard hit by the sinking lid on operating resources.

The reforms may not adequately recognise the extent to which ministers are dependent on their departments. In theory, ministers are in charge, for they hold the purse strings; as a practical matter, however, their performance is hostage to that of their departments. As much as ministers can accomplish their objectives by contracting for the purchase of outputs, they have vastly greater influence by building the capacity of their departments and steering them in new directions. Separated from departmental resources, most ministers are weak policy makers despite their contracting powers and control of appropriated funds. They depend on departments to get the job done.

In contrast to ministers, chief executives have been empowered by the reforms. They have been given virtual carte blanche to run their departments. The State Sector Act is intentionally brief in listing the powers and responsibilities of chief executives. Section 32 of the Act provides for each chief executive to be responsible "for a) the carrying out of the functions and duties of the Department ... and b) the tendering of advice to the appropriate Minister and other Ministers of the Crown; and c) the general conduct of the Department; and d) the efficient, effective, and economical management of the activities of the Department". Section 33 gives the chief executive managerial independence in all employment decisions, including appointment, promotion, transfer or termination of any employee. Section 34 gives chief executives "the powers necessary to carry out the functions, responsibilities, and duties" imposed by the State Sector Act or any other Act. They have personal and organisational responsibility for how well the department is performing; they are accountable for what they have contracted to do and for what they actually have done.

The process for appointing and assessing the performance of chief executives is as rigorous as it is time consuming. The State Sector Act establishes a trilateral appointment process. It provides for the State Services Commissioner to "appoint chief executives of departments and to negotiate conditions of employment", and for each relevant minister "to inform the Commission of any matter that the Minister wishes the Commission to take into account". Although the affected minister does not have a formal veto, the principle is established that a candidate should not be appointed against the objection of the minister and that a chief executive who has lost the confidence of the minister should not remain in the post.

Once appointed, the chief executive negotiates an annual performance agreement with the minister. This agreement specifies expectations concerning the chief executive's performance, emphasising matters to be given priority over the next year. Early performance agreements were improvised, and their form and content varied among departments; now, however, they are highly standardised. The current practice is to structure the agreement around the government's strategic result areas and the department's key result areas. The text of the agreement makes it clear that the chief executive accepts personal responsibility for each specified result. The chief executive also pledges in the agreement to produce the outputs contracted for in the purchase agreement and to uphold collective responsibilities.

Most chief executives see the key results specified in the agreement as a positive development, for they now have a clearer picture of what is expected of them. These key results also play a prominent role in assessing the performance of chief executives, many of whom prepare quarterly and annual checklists of progress made in achieving the key results and in producing the agreed outputs. Understandably, chief executives take care to show progress on as many key objectives as possible. They use the performance agreements as road maps for planning the department's work and measuring progress. This "management by checklist", may be a mixed blessing. It indicates that chief executives take the performance agreements seriously, but it may also narrow their perspectives and spur them to de-emphasise operational responsibilities not spelled out in the agreement.

The temptation to "manage by agreement" is reinforced by the demanding assessment process. Although chief executives may be appointed for terms of up to five years, their performance is reviewed each year. The annual review is conducted on the basis of three fundamental principles of New Zealand management: 1) the chief executive should be personally responsible for the department's performance; 2) performance expectations should be specified in advance; and 3) actual performance should be compared to the *ex ante* targets. The review takes up to six months, which means that one year's assessment follows on the heels of the last. Each chief executive has the burden of proof to document or certify that the terms of the purchase and performance agreements have been met. Each also prepares a self-assessment, which is supplemented by assessments from other relevant ministers, the three central agencies (the Treasury, the State Services Commission, and the Department of Prime Minister and Cabinet), and outside referees. The cost of operating this process is substantial, not only in financial terms, but also in the attention given it by chief executives and the State Services Commissioner, as well as in terms of the job stress induced by it. The costs are magnified by the large number of departments, each of which is headed by a chief executive who must go through this elaborate process.

This stress is reflected in high turnover and frequent vacancies. Many chief executives opt not to stand for reappointment, and some leave before their term has been completed. But stress is not due simply to the assessment process; it is inherent in the job. In New Zealand, managerial discretion and accountability are concentrated in the chief executive. To a degree that may be unmatched elsewhere, the chief executive is responsible for getting the job done and is blamed for organisational failures. Chief executives must act in ways that are at variance with the established culture of public administration. They must weed out weak managers; shed redundant workers; re-examine and sometimes sever long-standing relationships with suppliers; actively recruit from outside the civil service; negotiate the wages of senior managers; restructure operating units; abandon low-priority activities; contract in advance on outputs and resources; develop and promote the department's assets; develop and promote the department's priorities; take responsibility for the volume and quality of services; serve the minister and be responsive to his/her interests; negotiate employment, performance and purchase agreements; respond to numerous inquiries from Parliamentary committees and central agencies; participate in interdepartmental work; represent the department to the media and public; issue a stream of reports on the department's finances and performance; and much more. They must drive the department to be more productive, efficient and responsive. They must change the department and make it into a different, higher-performing organisation. They must, in short, be real managers who shape the department to their will. It is not easy for chief executives to do all these things well all of the time. In the fishbowl environment of New Zealand government, chief executives are observed and rated by peers, the media and others. This is an extraordinarily stressful position, and some leave it rather than continue to take the heat.

One of the chief executive's most important tasks is to recruit a corps of senior managers to run the department. This task obviously is more demanding in large, diversified departments than in small ones, but all chief executives have almost unlimited authority to decide whom to employ and the responsibilities to be assigned them. Most managers work under term contracts of up to five years, which may be renewed at the discretion of the chief executive. However, because of the turnover of chief executives and the age of many senior managers (many are bunched in the 45-55 age range) the contracts often are terminal appointments. As they near the end of their term, managers must decide (if the option is available) whether to continue under a new chief executive or to start a new career outside government. Many have moved into consultancies where their skills may still be available to departments through short-term contracts. There is some concern, therefore, that government may lose its most experienced managers and may face a shortage of talent in the future. Thus far, departments have had little difficulty recruiting skilled managers, but high unemployment during the early years of reform, a large pool of experienced managers trained in the old system but eager to adapt to the new one, ability to draw talent from the private sector into public service, and the excitement of working under the new regime assured an ample supply of qualified candidates. These conditions no longer prevail – for example, the proportion of senior managers drawn from private employment has diminished as the reforms have matured – and the government may have to increase its investment in human resources.

The State Sector Act envisioned that human resources would be developed by establishing a senior executive service (SES) as a pool of new management talent that would be, in the words of the Act, "a unifying force at the most senior level of the Public Service". The SES never really got off the ground, in part because many senior managers felt it would constrain their pay and work opportunities. Many were able to negotiate a better deal in individual employment contracts than might have been possible under SES.

One should not be surprised if public employment comes to resemble the structure of the private workforce, with more temporary, part-time and seasonal employees, and with more career instability and more movement between the public and private sectors. These trends have been encouraged by the Employment Contracts Act 1991 which terminated most differences in the conditions of public and private employment, as well as by the fragmentation of the civil service, and reforms that have put government operations on a more market-like basis. It certainly is easier than in the past to make mid-career moves between the public and private sectors. This mobility has led some departments to conclude that as they have greater opportunity to purchase personal services in the marketplace, they have less need to develop their own managers from within. If this attitude spreads, the services provided by public employees may come to be regarded as a commodity that can be purchased as needed.

MEASURING AND MONITORING PERFORMANCE

Accountability for performance revolves around the *ex ante* specification of future financial conditions and outputs, and the *ex post* reporting of results. Ministers and managers must agree in advance on financial performance (such as the condition of the balance sheet at year's end) and the outputs to be produced, the amounts to be spent on the agreed outputs, and the quality and timeliness of the work to be performed. This advance specification of performance enables ministers and managers to compare the volume, cost and quality of the outputs actually produced to the planned levels. This is the essence of accountability for performance in the New Zealand model – doing what was contracted at the agreed price and explaining variances between planned and actual results.

A necessary early step in this accountability regime is to specify the outputs of New Zealand government. The focus on outputs is in sharp contrast to the government's previous input-based appropriations and controls, as well as to the outcomes-oriented performance systems favoured by management reformers.

The Public Finance Act defines outputs as the goods and services produced by a department or by any other public or private supplier, and it provides for appropriations to be made by output classes which are defined as any "grouping of similar outputs". Much work has gone into defining the output classes, and while some refinements still are made each year, the structure has stabilised. Moreover, after some initial difficulty, considerable progress has been made in defining nondepartmental output classes. Most of these classes represent the activities conducted by departments and other entities; they typically describe the work performed for government, not the outputs produced. Many departments set aside an output class for policy advice and another for major administrative responsibilities, such as managing the contracts negotiated by the department.

The output classes are important because appropriations are made to them and departments manage and account for financial resources in terms of these classes. But efforts to make them into informative categories has led to an escalation in the number of appropriations. The Logan Review reported that the shift from broad Votes to outputs class appropriations had increased the number of separate appropriations from 56 in 1988/89 to 774 just three years later. Despite recommendations that output classes be consolidated, the number of such categories is now about the same as when the Logan Review was conducted. The large number of output classes may weaken managerial flexibility and complicate the always difficult task of apportioning overhead and other indirect costs among the various classes. There also is some danger that it will foster the same types of compliance behaviour and budgetary gamesmanship that flourished under input budgeting.

Although they are more numerous than some would like, the output classes are too broad to provide a basis for the purchaser-supplier relationship of ministers and managers. A 1992 interdepartmental working group recommended that chief executives specify the outputs to be supplied in annual agreements with ministers. These purchase agreements have gained quick acceptance and only three years after being introduced, they appear to have a secure niche in New Zealand public management. Practice concerning these agreements has not been standardised. Some ministers are aided in negotiations by purchase advisers; others sign the agreement without carefully reviewing its terms. Some ministers use the agreement to specify all the outputs to be delivered by the department; others use it principally as a means of impressing their priorities on the department. The most common pattern is one in which the chief executive drafts the agreement, and most of the outputs specified in the signed document are those proposed by the chief executive, but the minister inserts or modifies some items that she/he is interested in. Seen in this light, the usefulness of purchase agreements is not tested by whether ministers influence the entire document – they rarely do – but whether they get the department to accord priority to the outputs they care about. By this measure, purchase agreements have been quite useful.

These agreements vary in the detail included in them. Specification of outputs is taken by some to mean that the agreement should identify the volume of each output to be produced. According to this view, the purchase agreement should be treated as a firm contract (subject to renegotiation during the year) on the specific services to be delivered. Others, however, view the agreement more as an opportunity for periodic discussions between the minister and the chief executive on what the department is planning to do during the year. These types of agreements tend to have less detail. Although there may be considerable benefit in detailing the work to be performed during the year, trying to specify everything in advance may be counterproductive. Departments must be sufficiently supple to have the slack to deal with the surprises and unanticipated demands that arise during the year. Furthermore, over-specifying the outputs runs the risk that executives will "manage by the book", just as they did when inputs were centrally controlled.

Output data is prominently displayed in the estimates submitted to Parliament. At the outset, central agencies and departments had considerable difficulty designing output-oriented estimates. They wanted to provide useful information without overloading the documents in relatively unimportant detail. They had to identify the outputs, organise them into output classes, develop quantitative and qualitative measures of performance, and succinctly describe and measure the outputs. These steps entailed protracted negotiations involving the department, appropriate ministers, and the central agencies. The estimates went through major year-to-year revisions early in the process, but the design has stabilised, and only marginal adjustments are now made each year.

Measuring outcomes

Progress in measuring outputs has not been matched on the outcomes side of the ledger. The sharp distinction between outputs and outcomes has proved troublesome, as has the notion that managers should be responsible only for the former and ministers for the latter. The problem begins with the definition of outcomes in the Public Finance Act. Outcomes are "the impacts on, or the consequences for, the community of the outputs or activities of the government". This definition is grounded on a cause-effect relationship: outputs produce outcomes. This concept leads to the conclusion that ministers are responsible for outcomes because they are the purchasers of the outputs supplied to government. In fact, however, there is no inherent causal link of the two types of measures. Some outcomes may derive from specified outputs purchased by government; many do not. In the latter situation, which is the more common of the two, acquiring the right outputs does not ensure that the wanted outcomes will materialise.

Suppose, for example, that the average weight of new-born babies were declining or that infant mortality were rising. These adverse trends might be due to a number of factors, some of which may be beyond the control of government. Government can strive to achieve better outcomes by expanding prenatal care, disseminating advice on good personal care, distributing contraception to target populations, and other appropriate interventions. These activities may be useful, but still not countervail against poor nutritional habits and a surge in teenage pregnancies. Outcomes are the products of many factors, only some of which are within the competence of government. Specifying desired outcomes in advance and comparing these targets to actual results may lead to blaming politicians for matters over which they have little or no control. Politicians can try to side-step blame by not specifying the outcomes they hope to achieve. When this occurs, as it often has in New Zealand, accountability for outcomes breaks down.

The output-outcome distinction applied in New Zealand has had an additional defect. It seeks to separate government into two compartments: the political domain and management. Government at work, however, often blurs the distinction, as was noted in the earlier discussion of ministerial and managerial responsibility. It is with all its capacity and intelligence that government defines and pursues outcomes. Politicians contribute to the process, as do managers, policy advisors, service providers, and others. When managers tender advice, they do not desist from advising on outcomes, nor do politicians want them to. Public policy is enriched by continuing dialogue and feedback between politicians and managers, outputs and outcomes, policy and operations.

Even though New Zealand has not succeeded in establishing accountability for outcomes, the government must be aware of social conditions and trends. Regarding matters it deems important, it must know whether conditions are becoming more or less favourable, and it must act on the basis of this information. Seen in this light, outcomes are important indicators of direction. They are more useful in formulating policy than in maintaining accountability. They are powerful signals that show whether conditions are getting better or worse, and whether initiatives taken by the government have moved it closer to or further from stated objectives. Particular outcomes may not be the direct products of purchased outputs, but the government still has to take notice of them and develop appropriate responses. Even if it is not accountable, the government must take outcomes into account.

Strategic and Key Result Areas

The government has compensated for the inadequate development of out-come measures by devising new measures that emphasise its priorities and the directions it wishes to move toward.

Strategic and Key Result Areas (SRAs and KRAs) have been introduced in response to perceived shortcomings in the original reforms, in particular appre-hension that the collective interest had been slighted, difficulties in specifying and assessing outcomes, and the short-term orientation of policy. The SRAs represent medium-term objectives. They are the policy bridge between the government's long-term objectives (articulated in the 1993 document *Path to* 2010) and the one-year focus of departmental budgets, performance agreements and operating plans. Pursuant to the SRAs, each department establishes its key result areas, which form the basis for annual performance agreements.

The government has announced nine strategic areas. A close look at one of these shows how the SRAs may influence policies and budgets. SRA #2 is "Enter-prise and Innovation"; it communicates the government's intention to reinforce "a successful enterprise economy through maintaining and progressing an open trade environment..." This SRA identifies eight priorities, including policies that promote the open flow of goods, ideas and services between New Zealand and other countries; a simplified and viable fisheries management regime; gas and electricity reforms; and policies for the sustainable growth of tourism. These statements are broad, but they nevertheless indicate the direction the govern-ment wants to move.

The SRAs define objectives; the key result areas (KRAs) generally resemble output measures. Guidelines for the 1995/96 performance agreements advised chief executives to the major contributions they and their departments will make to the government's objectives over a 3-year period. These KRAs identify the goods and services to be provided in support of the SRAs, and although they, too, are broadly stated, the guidelines urged that progress toward achieving them should be expressed in observable and verifiable milestones. A review of per-formance agreements confirms that the KRAs and milestones have been cast in actionable terms. These documents provide a clear indication of the actions chief executives pledge to take in implementing the KRAs.

Few elements of the New Zealand reforms have attracted as much favour among ministers, chief executives and senior managers as have the SRAs and KRAs. These indicators have been rapidly and fully integrated into reformed public management; they are evidence of the malleability of the reforms and the capacity of government to adopt fresh ideas and reconsider old ones. Ministers like the SRAs/KRAs because they can more easily align their priorities to those of the government, and they can also claim additional resources on the argument that they are responding to the government's initiatives. Chief executives also like this new process because it gives them a clearer indication of the performance that is expected of them.

Monitoring and assessing performance

Monitoring performance against targets is a critical feature of managerial accountability. In contrast to other countries where *ex post* assessments take the form of programme evaluations, in New Zealand the paramount question is whether departments have delivered the agreed services at the specified cost. There is little formal programme evaluation underway, a characteristic that was criticised in the OECD Economic Survey quoted in the first section of this chapter.

Monitoring performance occurs both while the year is in progress and after it has been completed. Every purchase agreement has a monitoring and reporting provision that sets out the dates by which the chief executive will report to the minister on progress in producing the specified outputs. These typically are quarterly reports which identify and explain variances between agreed and actual performance and, when appropriate, proposed corrective action or modifications to the agreement. These reporting arrangements exert enormous influence on chief executives and their departments. As the financial year progresses, chief executives pay attention to the terms of the purchase agreement and organise the department's work to achieve as many of the targets as is feasible. Many managers keep checklists on the status of each item in the agreement. Typical checklist categories are "completed," "in progress" and "to be started". By the year's end, most chief executives can report that they have accomplished almost all of the agreed tasks. This checklist behaviour is welcomed by those who see it as evidence that managers are indeed accountable for what they do.

The annual report (which is audited) completes the annual accountability cycle. The Public Finance Act requires a series of financial and service performance statements in the annual report. These statements enable ministers and managers to compare planned and actual performance. The typical annual report consists of a narrative discussion of the department's operations during the year, and the required financial and service statements. Only these statements are not purely objective; the descriptive information typically seeks to portray the department in a favourable light.

MANAGING STATE FINANCES

Financial management is one of the successes of the New Zealand model. Within a short period (approximately 18 months), all departments shifted budgeting and accounting from a cash to an accrual basis, and applied commercial standards in preparing budgets and financial statements. Departments took responsibility for managing their own bank accounts and for preparing timely and accurate balance sheets and other financial statements. A capital charge has been imposed on the net assets of departments, and though this charge provoked considerable confusion and anxiety at the outset, most of the start-up problems have been overcome and the charge is now accepted as a practical means of encouraging departments to manage their physical and financial assets efficiently.

Perhaps the main problem encountered in the financial sphere is that departments feel that operating budgets often are set arbitrarily and often too low to enable them to carry out all their responsibilities. Downward pressure on operating resources has induced considerable job stress, as well as tension between the Treasury and some operating departments. The problem appears to be most serious in small departments, which face heavy burdens in meeting the various accountability requirements, and in departments with variable (and, typically, rising) workloads. The reforms have complicated the always difficult task of allocating public resources. On the one hand, resources are no longer explicitly allocated on the basis of input prices; on the other, cost accounting systems are not sufficiently developed to enable the government to appropriate funds on the basis of output costs.

In most regards, the New Zealand reforms give managers more discretion with respect to finances than is available in other countries. One major exception is that New Zealand still maintains strict annual financial control. It does not permit departments to carry forward unused operating funds from one financial year to the next. In New Zealand, unused funds are not treated as savings but as a surplus. The Public Finance Act stipulates that, except as agreed between the Minister of Finance and the Responsible Minister for a department, operating surpluses may not be retained. This provision has a simple rationale: the surplus belongs to the Crown, which provided the funds, and not to the department which produces the outputs. Whatever the conceptual basis of this practice, it may give departments the wrong message and incentives. It fosters a "use it or lose it" mentality, and most departments have become quite adept at spending just about all the money provided to them. Moreover, the reversion of operating surpluses to the Crown fails to distinguish between a surplus that is due to efficiency, or one that results from failure to complete all the planned work. It should be noted that the Treasury does not penalise departments for unspent funds; that is, it does not lower authorised baseline expenses for future years. When a department has an operating surplus, its baseline for the next several years is maintained at the same level as if all appropriated funds had been spent.

Role of the Treasury

The shift from input controls to output budgeting and appropriations has changed the role of the Treasury and other central agencies. Instead of directly managing human and financial resources, the new role of the central agencies is to manage the overall accountability system and to monitor and review departmental performance. The role of the Treasury is particularly important, and some claim that, despite the changes it has made, this organisation still exercises strong control over the departments. This claim may be due to the downward pressure that the Treasury has exerted on operational expenditures. Allocational rules that do not adjust running costs for inflation, that impose across-the-board percentage cutbacks, and that do not take sufficient account of rising workloads have been especially onerous on small departments that have little room for manoeuvre.

In recent years, the Treasury has sought to clarify its relations with departments by *a*) establishing core performance expectations that are common to all departments; *b*) issuing an annual relationship letting that sets out the particular matters the Treasury will review in assessing a particular department's performance; and *c*) issuing an annual feedback letter reviewing performance on the matters specified in the relationship letter. The core performance expectations identify the mutual obligation of the Treasury and departments to maintain open and trusting channels of communication, purchase and ownership requirements of all departments, and statutory obligations. This list is quite extensive and is revised each year to incorporate new requirements.

The relationship letter is a confidential communication from the Treasury to each chief executive specifying the matters to be given special attention during the year. This letter is drafted by the Treasury and finalised in negotiations with the affected department. The feedback letter comments on the department's performance concerning those matters specified in the relationship letter. It serves as the Treasury's audit or evaluation of the department's performance in selected areas. The feedback letter is confidential, but a copy is provided to the State Services Commissioner as input to the assessment of chief executive performance.

The budget process

The New Zealand reforms unwittingly telescoped the time frame for allocating resources and making other organisational decisions. In addition to the annual estimates, budget and appropriations, there are annual purchase and performance agreements, annual departmental forecast reports, annual business plans, and annual reports. This short time frame is intended to strengthen accountability for operations and resources, but it may also weaken the link between current actions (such as budget decisions) and future plans. The government does maintain a multi-year baseline, but allocation decisions are made on an annual basis.

Several steps have been taken to expand the time horizon for budgeting and other policy actions. These include the multi-year strategic and key result areas discussed earlier, optional (but increasingly popular) strategic plans, and a medium-term budget framework required by the Fiscal Responsibility Act 1994 (FRA). FRA requires the government to publish its medium-term fiscal strategy in a Budget Policy Statement several months before the budget is submitted to Parliament. This Statement announces the government's fiscal intentions over the next three years and explains any deviations from principles of sound fiscal management set forth in FRA.

The fiscal strategy deals with budget aggregates and macro-economic policy; it does not address particular estimates or programmes except when these may be affected by major policy initiatives. The government maintains a rolling baseline that covers the budget year and the following two financial years, and connects the fiscal strategy to particular votes. The baseline sets out, by vote, the agreed budget amounts for each of the three years; it is rebased every six months in the light of new economic forecasts and changes in government policy. Annual budget decisions revolve around bids to change the baseline or to reallocate resources within it. Changes to the baseline must be consistent with the government's medium-term strategy.

CONCLUDING COMMENTS

New Zealand's reformed state sector is an extraordinary accomplishment in modern public administration. New Zealand has been the first country to fully adopt accrual budgeting and accounting; the first to successfully implement output budgeting; the first to give managers full discretion in using inputs; the first to establish a comprehensive accountability regime. Being first means that certain deficiencies become apparent as reform takes hold. Some of these deficiencies have been discussed in this chapter. Perceived shortcomings in the original model have led to the SRA/KRA process, the use of purchase and performance agreements, a stronger interest in strategic planning, the medium-term perspective required by the Fiscal Responsibility Act, and other adjustments. Undoubtedly, additional changes will be made in the years ahead, perhaps by way of encouraging programme evaluation and clearer specification of outcomes. The business of management improvement is never done, not even in a country where reform is guided by powerful ideas and a comprehensive blueprint.

5

SWEDEN

Management reform in Sweden has moved in the same general direction as has reform in the other countries discussed in this report. The basic formula is that less central regulation of the details of expenditure should be accompanied by more agency accountability for results. Change has been less dramatic than elsewhere because basic institutional arrangements have remained intact and no new organs have been established. But institutional stability has coexisted with procedural change, for the government has adjusted the reforms in response to somewhat disappointing progress. Nevertheless, the key ideas and objectives of reform are the same now as they were almost a decade ago: to transform state agencies that spend resources on the basis of *ex ante* controls into entities that manage their resources to produce the results expected of them.

Progress has been uneven, especially as regards the transformation of the budget process into a means of managing for results. In fact, the government has been impelled to loosen the dependence of reform on budget actions. Nowadays, it places more emphasis on annual reports and audits and less than it once did on periodic budget decisions. Yet there also are encouraging signs of a positive impact on the management and performance of state agencies. In assessing progress, one should note that, although the reforms were conceived in the mid-1980s, full implementation was not reached until the early 1990s. When this study was undertaken, all agencies had operated under the new regime for only about two years. It should also be noted that the financial management reforms are not the only instruments of change available to the Swedish government. Ad *hoc* committees, programme evaluation, effectiveness auditing, and legislative action are heavily used channels for improving the public sector.

The Swedish model of reform relies more on discussion and guidance than on competition or contract, more on public institutions than on markets, more on confidence that public managers will do well if given the opportunity than on incentives that reward efficiency. The reforms have less to do with reducing the cost of government (though there is some of that) than with spurring agencies to be efficient in accomplishing approved objectives with authorised resources. The reforms concentrate on operating costs, but they are animated by the expectation that the effectiveness of programmes also will be improved by establishing performance targets and letting agencies manage their own operations. They depend on Sweden's distinctive separation of ministries that are responsible for policy decisions from state agencies that spend most public funds and carry out the programmes assigned to them. This division of governmental responsibility between ministries and agencies is critical to the successful implementation of the reforms. Finally, the reforms have been inspired by Sweden's characteristic optimism that the machinery and operations of government can be perfected to improve the effectiveness of public programmes and overall social conditions.

RESULTS-ORIENTED BUDGETING

Prior to reform, the government gave agencies technical instructions for preparing annual budgets. It then reviewed the detailed requests and recommended spending levels to Parliament. After appropriations were voted, the government issued detailed instructions, in a *Regleringsbrev*, on how available funds were to be used. The instructions typically itemised the various categories of expenditure (personnel, premises, equipment and other items) and set limits and other conditions on the amounts to be spent on each category. Each agency was bound to these conditions in implementing its budget. Budget documents sometimes indicated the work to be done or set forth other measures of performance, but the predominant focus was on the items of expenditure. At all stages of budgeting, there was inordinate attention to administrative costs rather than to the much larger amounts allocated to transfer payments and other programme expenditures. The close review of operating expenditures was repeated year after year, despite the fact that the government had successfully imposed a "cheese-slicer" rule that constrained increases in these resources to approximately 2 per cent below inflation-adjusted spending levels. Centralised control of spending details did not, however, prevent agencies from exceeding their budgets and spending more than had been provided by the government. In exercising strong control of the details of expenditure, the government had relatively weak control of total spending.

The reconstructed budget process emphasises control of total agency expenditure rather than of the details. It focuses on outputs rather than inputs, on the next three years and not just on the financial year immediately ahead, on demanding that agencies manage resources to produce the results agreed in budget decisions and not just to satisfy externally imposed rules and restrictions. The following excerpt from a 1993 Ministry of Finance report, *Management of Government Administration and Financial Conditions for State Agencies*, spells out the principles and objectives of reform:

- The first purpose is for the activities of the agency to be reviewed as a whole, and for the level of the budget to serve as an expression of the agreed and expected level of ambition for its activities. The new budget principles mean that all the activities of the agency, with its various types of resource, will be budgeted on an aggregated basis and in the same manner.

- Agencies which receive their funds in an appropriation frame are free to allot the total financial resources granted by Government. Normally, there will be no specific restrictions on what proportion of the total general budget which is allot-ted to the agency shall be used for wages, for example, or premises.

The new flexibility allows agencies to retain resources gained through efficiency improvements beyond those targeted in the budget. The government's position on this matter is quite firm; if agencies were forced to surrender these savings, they would be penalised for being more efficient. Moreover, "it must be possible for decisions on efficiency improvements to be made to the greatest extent possible by the agency concerned, within given financial limits, without needing to obtain the approval of Government."

The restructured process makes agencies fully responsible for managing their budgets, even to the extent of permitting them to carry over unused funds from one year to the next and to pre-spend (within certain limits) a portion of the next year's appropriation. Each agency's budgeted funds are deposited in an interest-bearing account for which the agency is responsible. It may borrow funds (within authorised limits) from the National Debt Office to finance the acquisition of fixed assets. It must repay such loans with interest out of the operating account. It also pays interest if the rate of spending is faster than was budgeted and earns interest if the rate is slower. Each agency is thus fully responsible for managing its cash resources and operating within the cash limit set by its appropriation frame. Each agency normally has a single frame covering all running costs, though it may have additional frames for certain programme expenditure or notional frames for expenditures financed through user charges or other receipts that are netted against gross spending. In the new scheme, agencies are no longer compensated for in-year cost increases above the amount provided in the appropriation.

The new flexibility and responsibility given agencies is accompanied by an expanded budget process that is oriented to the outputs and results to be produced over a three-year period. Triennial budgeting was pilot-tested in the mid-1980s and expanded throughout government near the end of the decade. After several years of experience, in which all agencies went through a fixed three-year cycle, the government adjusted the length of the cycle to each agency's circumstances. In launching the reforms, the government classified state agencies into three groups, with one group entering a triennial budget cycle each year. When it enters the cycle, an agency is expected to undergo much more intensive scrutiny than was normally conducted in the conventional annual budget process.

As it prepared for three-year decisions, each agency would assess its work and accomplishments during the previous five years and consider the resources and activities planned for the next three years. These evaluations would be guided by general instructions issued to all agencies, as well as by special instructions addressed by the relevant ministry to each agency scheduled for in-depth review. For example, an agency might be directed to devise new methods of measuring performance or to emphasise different priorities than those pursued in the past. In the logic of reform, after an agency completes this assessment, it and the government would decide on the objectives, activities, and resources for the next three years. In this way, the government hoped, budgeting would be expanded from an incremental process that typically makes only marginal adjustments in activities and resources into a fuller opportunity for reviewing and changing the objectives, performance and resources of agencies. As long as it kept within available resources, the government declared, "it should be possible for a growing proportion of operative decisions to be made directly by the agency concerned, provided that the financial limits are known. Within these limits, the agency then has responsibility to formulate targets for its own production, to decide on the allocation of resources, etc." Although appropriations continue to be made one year at a time, agencies submit simplified budget requests during the intermediate years of the cycle unless they (or the government) want to change the volume or type of activities or supplement the available resources.

The *quid pro quo* for giving agencies managerial discretion is to hold them accountable for results. In the course of the deeper scrutiny at the start of each triennial cycle, each agency would have to set forth the results expected to be produced with available resources. During each year of the cycle, it would have to report on performance, and at the conclusion of the cycle a new in-depth review would be undertaken. By means of performance measures and other data, agencies would have to stipulate expected results and then compare what they had actually accomplished to plans. Finally, the National Audit Office would review agency performance measures and reports to assess the reliability of the data and the effectiveness of agency operations.

GENERAL ASSESSMENT OF REFORM

In assessing the progress of reform, one should acknowledge two features of Swedish public administration. First, before the budget reforms were launched, public management was less centrally controlled in Sweden than in other countries. Swedish agencies have long had a great deal of managerial freedom in conducting their activities, and they also have exhibited considerable interest in results and performance. The very centrality of government in the daily lives of Swedes has sensitised agencies to the importance of producing expected results. Hence, while reform may have been less far-reaching than elsewhere, fewer dramatic changes were needed to orient managers to performance. Second, reform is an ongoing process in Swedish government. At any time, dozens of reforms are under way, many dealing with programmes and policies, but many also with administrative organisation. More than any other country studied in this report, Sweden relies on *ad hoc* committees (or commissions), convened either by the government or Parliament, to examine current practices or issues and to recommend reforms. During expansionary times, hundreds of *ad hoc* committees were at work. There are fewer these days, but they still are a potent force in the adjustment of public policies or organisations. The committees are consensus-building devices for initiating new programmes or altering older ones. They reflect confidence in the capacity of government to improve society, not by uprooting existing policies but by fine-tuning them on the basis of experience and fresh ideas. This process gives an optimistic and incremental tinge to public management in Sweden.

In the 1985-95 period, this writer was told, about one hundred agencies – approximately one-third of the total – were significantly reorganised. At every agency visited for this study there was evidence of recent reform. The National Rail Administration was established in 1988 as part of a sweeping reform that set up a separate enterprise for railway transport. In the early 1990s, the Forensic Medicine Agency was created by merging previously separate medical specialities; in 1992, the National Roads Administration was assigned highway safety, which had been the responsibility of a separate agency; in 1992, also, the National Board for Spent Nuclear Fuel was abolished and its work was assigned to the Nuclear Power Inspectorate; in 1994, administration of housing allowances was transferred to the Social Insurance Board.

Financial management reform has been part of this ferment, yet different. Unlike reforms initiated by special committees, it has not been *ad hoc* or opportunistic. Rather, the quest for improvement has been institutionalised in the recurring work of budget formulation. Reformers have sought to exploit two features of government budgeting: 1) its prominence in allocating resources; and 2) a cycle of procedures that are repeated with little change year after year. The initiation of each three-year cycle would, it was expected, be the occasion for making strategic decisions on the objectives and direction of affected agencies. The decisions would be much more than the marginal adjustments conventionally made in annual budgeting; they would redirect agencies, question old priorities and establish new ones, and they would target resources to the results sought by government. But if this was the hope, the reality may be somewhat more modest. The routines of budgeting do not readily stretch to accommodate broader purposes. Reform has encountered an old conflict between doing things repetitively, which is what budgeting excels at, and the strategic perspective that the reformed budget process was to encourage. Budget reformers in Sweden have relearned an old lesson – that the questioning of results and purposes cannot always be done according to the calendar and deadlines of budgeting.

The reforms were conceived in the mid-1980s, during what turned out to be a brief interlude in the fiscal crises that beset Sweden at the start and end of the decade. By the early 1980s, the fault lines in the Swedish economy were quite visible: growth rates well below that of Europe and the OECD community, persistent trade imbalances, a progressive rise in public expenditure and in the tax burden, deteriorating terms of trade, and periodic devaluation of the krona. Following a large devaluation in 1982, and modest changes in tax and spending policies, the economy recovered, the fiscal condition of the public sector steadily improved, and budgetary balance was achieved late in the decade. It was in this environment that the Social Democratic Government launched the financial management reforms. But fiscal improvement was only temporary, due more to an overheated economy that veiled chronic imbalances than to structural adjustments in government policy. When the bubble burst at the start of the 1990s, the country was plunged into its deepest economic crisis since the Depression, with soaring unemployment and interest rates, and a public sector budget deficit approaching 13 per cent of GDP. The election of 1991 brought a change of government, but the course of financial management reform was not affected. The new right-of-centre government moved the reforms from pilot-testing to full implementation. This commitment to reform was continued by the Social Democratic government which was formed after the 1994 election. Thus, neither economic nor political turbulence interrupted the progress of reform. Financial management improvement, like most other Swedish reforms, was more a matter of national consensus than of political ideology.

The fiscal crisis, which lingered after the economy began to recover, sharpened awareness at both political levels and in the civil service that state agencies could no longer expect enhancements in operating resources; they would have to make do with less. Even when asked to do more, they would have serious resource constraints. In fact, most of the agencies visited for this study have experienced staff reductions since the reforms were initiated and all expect the attrition of staff and other operating resources to persist in the years ahead. Officials in these agencies express the view that their newly acquired managerial flexibility has facilitated adjustment to the budgetary constraints and has enabled them to maintain staff morale and activity levels. In most of the agencies, however, the financial management reforms are adjudged to be less salient in improving managerial performance than have been other decisions taken outside the budget process, such as reorganisation and policy changes initiated by ad hoc commissions. In discussions with agency officials, one senses that financial management reform, though welcomed, has been overwhelmed by the deep fiscal and economic crisis. There is widespread awareness, in both ministries and agencies, that the efficiencies and savings accruing from these reforms do not make much of a dent in the budget deficit. From the perspective of the government, improving management is less urgent than reducing the deficit. The crisis has made it hard for the government to take and keep three-year resource decisions. With the fiscal outlook so dire, the government has been impelled to budget one year at a time. In interviews, some agency officials complained that the 1995/96 budget required them to reduce administrative expenses by 11 per cent over the next $3^1/_2$ years without any corresponding diminution in output. They understood the compelling need for austerity, but they nevertheless felt that it weakens multi-year commitments.

Progress in rationalising public management is dependent on the distinctive division of responsibilities noted earlier: ministries guide policy and agencies implement programmes. The reforms cannot work as expected if ministries do not issue guidance on objectives and results or if agencies do not operate according to the guidance given them. In blueprint, the relationship seems to be ideal for results-oriented budgeting. Rather than having to establish new arrangements and relationships, as has been the case elsewhere, the Swedish government needs only to shift the basis of guidance from inputs to outputs. However, the relationship between ministries and agencies has been one of the weak links in the reform process. To understand why, one must explain how the two sides operate. The ministries are very small; they average only a little more than one hundred staff each. There are only about one dozen ministries, compared to approximately three hundred state agencies, plus many more county and local boards. Thus the average ministry is responsible for about two dozen agencies. Many agencies are small, but some are very large, with thousands of employees and vast programme responsibilities. The agencies deliver, either directly or through county and local units, almost all of the services financed by state expenditure.

For example, the Ministry of Health and Social Affairs is responsible for almost 30 per cent of total state expenditure. But almost all of its funds and the delivery of most of the services under its purview are entrusted to the National Social Insurance Board, an agency with 15 000 employees and offices throughout the country. This and other agencies operate in a twilight zone between independence and compliance. It is a fundamental tenet of Swedish governance that ministries may not intervene in the administrative operations of agencies; they may establish general policy but may not become involved in particular cases. It is also a fundamental tenet that agencies must operate according to the rules and prescriptions set for them by the government. In being both independent and compliant, agencies must distinguish between politics and administration. This distinction sometimes is fuzzy at the edges – after all, agencies do influence policy and ministries do sometimes become involved in administrative matters –

but it nevertheless works reasonably well. The two sides understand and accept their respective roles. Agencies do generally operate according to the policy guidelines set for them; they do not cavalierly ignore or defy policy instructions.

The financial management reforms assume that ministries will eagerly adopt the enlarged role of providing guidance on objectives and results in lieu of the traditional regulations on inputs and administrative details. But the ministries have been slow in taking up the new assignment. They have made much more progress in divesting the old controls than in steering agencies on the results to be achieved or in following up on actual performance. If all that reform entailed were divestiture of the old controls, it would already show significant success. The *Regleringsbrev* are much slimmer than they were a decade ago, and agencies have substantial flexibility in the use of funds. But this is the easy part of reform. The difficult work of making resource decisions on the basis of expected performance, then reporting on results and following up with corrective action lags behind. Although there are differences across government, both ministry and agency staff agree that this essential feature of reform has not developed as expected. It appears that the main problems lie in the issuance of budget and policy guidance by ministries and in their capacity to monitor agency progress in achieving the results for which resources have been provided.

Ministries face a number of impediments in fulfilling the role expected of them. One is that senior officials concentrate on political matters – relations with other ministries, cabinet business and pending legislation – rather than on the management of agencies. No senior official is responsible for overseeing agency activities. A working group on reform recommended in early 1995 that each ministry have a "managing director" who would be placed immediately below political levels and would be responsible for providing guidance to agencies and monitoring results.

But giving agency management higher visibility and priority is not the only issue that stands in the way of effective policy guidance from ministries. A more serious one may be the mismatch in staff resources. The ministries are so small and some agencies so large that the former are unable to formulate objectives, issue instructions and respond to data on performance. This imbalance is evident in the Ministry of Transport and Communications, whose eighty-person staff is responsible for agencies that employ 120 000 workers.

In practice, the relationship between ministries and agencies is less clearly drawn than is indicated by the split between politics and administration. The relationship is based on discussion and consensus rather than on formal negotiation and decision. Each side brings to the table the matters it wishes to discuss – either can suggest the performance targets to be pursued for the next year or the special reporting requirements to be imposed on the agency. The word used by several officials interviewed for this study is dialogue – a word that connotes give and take, an informal relationship in which neither side is wholly in control or wholly compliant. The word dialogue cropped up to describe how budget frames and performance targets are selected, as well as how objectives are defined and progress measured. Dialogue conveys a less formal relationship than one in which the ministry prescribes and the agency produces. But although each side contributes to the dialogue, there is an impression that the agencies have the upper hand in the discussions. They know more about their programmes and they care more about them; they have the skills and the resources to collect data on performance; and they generally have the skills to ensure that the measures selected are within reach. From the agency perspective, there is a risk that, especially on matters of high political salience, the ministry will insist on results that the agency cannot achieve with the resources at hand or over which it has weak control. Overall, however, the dialogue comports well with the Swedish model. It is a relationship based on consensus and trust. The dialogue softens the hard edge of measurement and reinforces the independence of agencies while enabling both parties to talk about results.

THE BUDGET PROCESS

In blueprint, the reforms contemplate that the dialogue between ministries and agencies should revolve around multi-year budget decisions. As described earlier, it was initially expected that at the start of its three-year cycle, each agency would prepare an in-depth assessment of past accomplishments and future objectives, and that these would be based on specific guidelines provided by the cognisant ministry. Thus far, the only feature of the reformed process to be significantly revised is the three-year cycle. In fact, however, there has been a marked de-emphasis of the budget as the instrument for assessing results in the light of resources. There has been a corresponding increase in reliance on annual reports and formal audits. In addition, *ad hoc* commissions continue to be an important means of channelling reforms into government.

There are five stages or "transactions" at which planned or actual results are intended to feed into the budget: 1) at the start of the multi-year cycle; 2) in the formulation of budget frame decisions; 3) in the *Regleringsbrev* issued after appropriations are approved; 4) in the review of annual reports and other data on results; and 5) in the comprehensive assessment at the conclusion of the multi-year cycle. It was expected that the lengthening of the budget cycle and the infusion of a results orientation would transform budgeting from a routine process for making marginal adjustments in resources into a fuller opportunity to redirect government policies, programmes and resources. Experience to date indicates that recurring decisions on administrative resources may not afford a sufficiently open opportunity for considering non-incremental policy changes. Most decisions on the operating budget entail marginal adjustments in resources. At each stage the government has had limited success in generating a robust examination of intentions or results.

The problem begins at the first stage – preparation of in-depth requests. The government has found that the three-year cycle is too short for undertaking a probing assessment of some agencies but too long for committing resources to other agencies. In 1992, the government proposed three-year frames for a little more than half of the agencies reviewed that year. In some cases, the in-depth analyses submitted by agencies were not of sufficient quality for the government to make a long-term decision; in other cases, the agencies were in the midst of *ad hoc* reviews outside the budget process. The government has concluded that in-depth reviews should no longer be conducted on a fixed schedule. Instead, it specifies each year in which agencies shall be subject to such review, provided, however, that not more than six years elapse between in-depth assessments.

The rigidity of the cycle has not been the only problem encountered at this stage. Ministries, for reasons already mentioned, have had difficulty formulating guidelines for the reviews and agencies have been reluctant to undertake the probing assessments that might call their own programmes or even their continuing existence into question. The Agency for Administrative Development has concluded that for many agencies it is difficult to relate the results of their activities to the resources allotted to them. In many cases, the connection between demands for new resources and the conclusions in the analyses of results is by no means evident. In many cases, the in-depth budget requests are far too extensive and opaque to provide an adequate planning basis for the government office. Not insignificant amounts of the information in the in-depth budget requests lack relevance for the government's decision-making.

This finding touches on the second stage of budgeting – decisions on resources. Despite the virtual elimination of central controls on the items of expenditure, agen-cies still compile their budgets by estimating the cost of these items. The annual budget bill submitted to Parliament runs about 2 500 pages, about the same as it did before reform. There has been no significant reduction in the details crammed into it. The government recognises that Parliament has not been a partner in the development of results-oriented budgeting, but it hopes that further reforms to be undertaken in 1995 will focus legislative attention on more aggregated issues rather than on spending details.

The budget reform was expected to reorient the *Regleringsbrev* from a control document to policy guidance. This document is critical to agencies because it determines the resources they have to spend and sets conditions on use of the resources. This "approval document" is much slimmer now than before the reforms because the itemisation of inputs has been eliminated, but it is not yet sufficiently focused on outputs. A 1995 Ministry of Finance report, *Annual Performance Accounting and Auditing in Sweden*, asserts that this document "has taken on more importance in the management of government agencies. It must include details of objectives, performance requirements, resources and framework conditions". The approval document is the principal means of formally communicating a ministry's expectations on performance to each of its agencies. Thus far, however, the performance requirements have typically been general, though the approval document often specifies reporting demands or other tasks to be undertaken during the fiscal year. The government hopes that as ministries gain experience, they will be more confident in prescribing the results to be achieved.

ANNUAL REPORTS

As the importance of budget procedures as a means of reorienting management to results has diminished, the government has placed greater weight on the annual report submitted by each agency shortly after the close of the fiscal year. These reports have been given a broader role, and demands on agencies to monitor and assess the results of operations have been made more stringent. Furthermore, the National Audit Office (NAO) has been given a prominent role in auditing the annual reports and in advising the government concerning the reliability of agency assessments of their performance. As spelled out in a 1993 ordinance, each annual report has two parts: financial statements and the results of operations. The NAO audit covers both parts of the report.

The financial statements (which include a balance sheet, income statement, an appropriation report, and a statement of changes in financial position) must conform to generally accepted accounting practice. According to the NAO, most agencies have made significant progress in putting their financial accounts on an accrual basis and in maintaining the records needed for the preparation of the financial statements.

Progress has been slower and more uneven in reporting on performance. The 1993 ordinance prescribes that annual reports for each agency shall report and comment on the result of operations in relation to the objectives. By result is meant the outputs of the agency and the measurable effects of these outputs. For each branch of operations, the agency shall report specifically on the development of the result in terms of volume, income, costs and quality. Significant deviations from the goal shall be explained. The result shall be compared with the result for the previous three years. The ordinance further stipulates that in analysing the result of operations, output and the effects of its operations shall be evaluated in relation to the goals of operations and overall objectives.

In the first years that the expanded annual reports have been required, agencies generally have had more success in complying with financial reporting rules than with those pertaining to performance. Many annual reports have been descriptive, with performance data, especially pertaining to workload and activities, sprinkled throughout. Few agencies have yet mastered the technique of systematically assessing results in the light of objectives. The NAO recognises that generally accepted accounting principles are as yet undeveloped with regard to performance reporting. The NAO also recognises that, in contrast to financial reporting, it is not possible to consistently apply simple 'black or white' criteria when evaluating a performance report. Performance must be assessed in terms of a particular agency's objectives and programmes.

Despite the difficulty of assessing performance, the annual reports provide substantial evidence that agencies have been responsive to the new demands. The National Social Insurance Board devotes almost an entire chapter in its 1993/94 report to an assessment of whether it has achieved the government's target of reducing the incapacity rate for sickness and disability one day below the previous year's level. The report provides trend data on incapacity and it estimates the extent to which changes in rules and other developments have affected the rate. The report concludes that the results were comparable to the goals laid down by the government. But it also notes that, in this and other areas of social policy, the outcomes are partly beyond its control and are affected by general economic and social trends.

Agencies also consider performance failures in their reports. The Swedish Nuclear Power Inspectorate's 1992/93 report took note of serious safety deficiencies at one of its facilities that prevented it from meeting workload targets for the year. The report states that measures to improve safety have been implemented, but it does not describe the actions taken nor does it assess the risk of similar breakdowns occurring in the future. This report was prepared for the first year that expanded annual reports were required. There is reason to believe that, under prodding from the auditors, many agencies have taken steps to upgrade the content and quality of their reports. A comparison of the 1992 and 1993 reports of the National Roads Administration provides evidence of the advances made within that short period of time. The 1992 report dealt mostly with financial results and the agency's organisation. It was adorned with graphic data on accidents, pollution, and other relevant facts, but no effort was made to analyse this material or to relate it to the agency's results. The 1993 report, by contrast, began with a systematic, albeit brief, statement of performance in terms of the five objectives set by the government for the Roads Administration: availability, efficiency, road safety, environmental quality and regional balance. The report summarises each objective, the measures used to assess performance, and the results achieved. Subsequent sections of the report summarise results in each region of the country and in each division of the agency.

An annual report is of little value unless it is used by the agency in upgrading its performance or by the government in making policy decisions and allocating resources. Several agency officials asserted in interviews that the annual reports are only of historical value because they are produced after the fiscal year is over, too late to influence the actions of managers. Annual reports in government, as in the private sector, are prepared for external users. The annual report is not likely to be as forthcoming or as timely as internal documents, such as variance reports, produced during the year. In preparing the annual report, an agency has a strong incentive to present itself in a favourable light, concentrating on the successes and saying rather less about the difficulties and disappointments. Most ministries lack the capacity to comb through the reports submitted by their agencies and to act on the basis of the information contained in these documents. It is likely, therefore, that agencies will be the main users of the reports and that the process of reporting on results will be more valuable to them than will the reports themselves.

The government has sought to elevate the prominence of these reports by entrusting the NAO with responsibility for auditing them. The NAO's role in performance auditing probably surpasses that assigned the national audit authority in any other country. The NAO's extraordinary role is anchored in two decades of experience in programme evaluation. Like other Swedish agencies, the NAO straddles the line between independence and compliance. In conducting audits, the NAO affirms its independence by acting on the basis of established professional principles and practices. It alone decides how audits are to be done. But the NAO also is directly accountable to the Ministry of Finance; much of its work, particularly in financial management reform and performance reporting, is conducted pursuant to instructions from the ministry.

Prior to budget reform, the NAO operated on the periphery of the Swedish public administration. It was situated in an outlying area of Stockholm, some distance from the centre of government. Its evaluations and reports were given respectful attention, but they were not directly fed into the budget process or other policy decisions. In the early 1990s, the NAO was relocated to central Stockholm, near the ministries, and it was assigned the task of auditing the annual reports. These moves are designed to link the NAO's work more closely to government decisions on resources and programmes. The NAO's auditors review both the financial statements and performance claims; they may "qualify" an annual report – that is, they may find that material deficiencies in the report prevent them from certifying it as a true and fair account of the agency's finances or results. In 1994, the NAO qualified twenty-nine annual reports, approximately 10 per cent of those submitted by agencies. It found, for example, that the 1993/94 annual report of the National Social Insurance Board lacked sufficient information on performance and did not adequately analyse results in relation to goals. The fact that the NAO did not object to most reports did not mean that it was satisfied with them. The NAO took account of the limited experience of agencies in reporting on performance. If it had not, many more qualified audit reports would have been issued. The NAO recognises that much additional work must be done in establishing and applying performance standards. Although it has a staff of almost one hundred performance auditors (in addition to those engaged in financial auditing and financial management), the NAO has encountered substantial difficulty in auditing results. "The audit cannot give the same guarantee of reliability for a Performance Report as for the other parts of the annual report. It is important to diminish the 'gap in expectations' between what the audit can actually guarantee and what the parties interested in the audit expect."

The NAO audit has at least three interested parties: the affected agency, the ministry to which the agency is responsible, and the Ministry of Finance. Each receives a copy of the audit report. When an agency's annual report has been qualified, it must respond by indicating the steps it is taking to remedy the deficiencies. Thus, after the NAO objected to its annual report, the National Social Insurance Board thoroughly reviewed its operations and adjusted its internal controls and other procedures to improve the quality of its data. The NAO believes that the threat of having their reports qualified has prodded agencies to do better job in accounting for results.

But if preparation of the annual reports has been a useful exercise for agencies, evidence is still lacking that ministries rely on the reports in steering the agencies responsible to them. Nor is there yet much evidence of use of the reports in preparing or reviewing budget requests. The annual reports and audits are supposed to form a feedback loop in which the results of operations inform the next year's budget decisions. Although these reports and audits may provide a more objective picture of agency goals and performance than is typically available in conventional budget requests, it nevertheless remains to be demonstrated that the responsible ministry or the Ministry of Finance will rely on the performance data in allocating resources. The annuality of the budget and the need to act on a comprehensive set of issues in a short period of time may impel budgetmakers to settle for marginal adjustments rather than more sweeping resource decisions. Budgeting may prove to be as inhospitable to the probing analyses set forth in annual reports and audits as it has been to the in-depth reviews prescribed for triennial budget frames and earlier reforms.

Indeed, the most fruitful application of the annual reports and audits may be found in *ad hoc* arrangements, such as the uniquely Swedish reliance on study committees. These may be a more effective force for strategic adjustment than that provided by the recurring work of budget preparation and review. One should not be surprised or disappointed if public sector reform in Sweden accomplishes some of its most salient objectives by taking a different route than the one chose almost a decade ago.

6

UNITED KINGDOM

Since 1988, management reform in the United Kingdom has advanced under the aegis of the "Next Steps" initiative. This initiative entails the establishment of executive agencies responsible for the delivery of services with a measure of independence from the departments in which they are located. The launching of an agency follows a period of negotiation during which a Framework Document spelling out the authority under which it will operate, expected resources, and targets for performance is formulated. Each agency is headed by a chief executive, who is employed, usually for a fixed term, pursuant to a performance contract which sets forth salary, working conditions and responsibilities.

By the start of 1995, more than one hundred executive agencies had been established and another sixty-four were in candidate status. Almost two-thirds of the civil service (353 000) were employed in executive agencies and almost 100 000 worked in the candidate agencies. These numbers include two large departments – Inland Revenue and Customs and Excise – which are not formally part of the Next Steps initiative but which have organised regional and other offices on Next Steps principles. Inasmuch as about 10 per cent of the civil service is employed in central policy-making and management operations of departments (and therefore are not within the ambit of Next Steps), while another 10 per cent perform tasks for which this initiative is deemed to be inappropriate, the coverage of Next Steps is near to full potential.

In addition to Next Steps, a variety of related and supporting initiatives have been undertaken thus far in the 1990s. These include reform of the civil service, resource (accrual) accounting and budgeting, efficiency plans, and fundamental reviews of departments. Since the first Thatcher government in 1979, the public sector has witnessed efficiency scrutinies, the Financial Management Initiative (FMI), delegated budgeting, running cost controls, Next Steps agencies, the Citizen's Charter, market testing, and more. In addition to these innovations in central government, major strides have been taken to restructure local authorities, the National Health Service, and the provision of education. Each reform has brought new requirements for data and documents, so that central government institutions now negotiate framework documents, establish performance targets, issue business and corporate plans as well as annual reports and financial accounts, measure results and evaluate agencies, and generate other means of holding public managers accountable for resources and results.

The drive to transform public management has also been stimulated by shrinkage in the size of the civil service and downward pressure on running costs. The civil service numbered approximately 700 000 when Margaret Thatcher took office in 1979; by the mid-1990s, it had shed almost 200 000 posts. (The civil service comprises only a portion of total public employment in the United Kingdom; it does not include the National Health Service, local authorities, and certain other bodies.) The staff reductions have been propelled by the privatisation of enterprises and by reductions in the running costs allowed spending units.

The reforms have been shaped by two coexisting but different conceptions of a transformed public sector. One is the idea that services should be provided through markets or market-type arrangements; the other is the idea that public organisations should be managed by persons who are given the resources and authority to provide the services for which they are accountable. Markets and management are powerful forces in the reforms that have swept through British government. Elements of both can be found in the Thatcher-Major initiatives. The drive to marketise the public sector is most closely associated with prior options and market testing, discussed later in this chapter. These have been among the most controversial reforms, for they presume that primary reliance should be placed on business for the provision of services, and that government should be engaged only to the extent that private arrangements are not suitable. Moreover, when government does have a role, it should operate to the extent feasible along commercial lines. Marketisation has also been associated with the competitive recruitment of chief executives who work under contract, as well as with framework documents that spell out the relationship of executive agencies and parent departments.

Yet it is not principally markets and contracts that have driven reform, but a managerial ethic rooted in the idea that public services should be organised so as to ensure that they are effectively delivered at low cost. Putting this idea into practice has led to initiatives that purport to give managers a free hand to run operations within the policy guidance and resources provided, and that require managers to be notified in advance of the performance expected of them. This ethic strongly implies that managers should have the freedom to decide whom to hire and how much to pay them, as well as discretion to spend on particular items within agreed budgets. The managerial spirit thrives, reformers insist, when those served by agencies are regarded as customers rather than as clients, and when public agencies make explicit the standards of service provided to customers.

These managerial imperatives led to the inauguration of Next Steps agencies in 1988. By all accounts, this reform has been the single most prominent change during the Thatcher-Major years. But while Next Steps may be viewed as the triumph of managerialism, some see it as a way-station along the road to privatisation. It is true that to the extent that government agencies operate along commercial lines, they become increasingly ripe for privatisation. Thus far, however, few Next Steps agencies have been turned over to private hands, though some have been prepared for privatisation. Next Steps is not the last step in the modernisation process, but most future reforms are likely to take place within the boundaries of the public sector.

ANTECEDENTS TO NEXT STEPS

The Thatcher government was in power for almost a decade before it initiated Next Steps. Prior to Next Steps, the government tried to improve public management by means of efficiency scrutinies, the Financial Management Initiative, and delegated budgeting. The scrutinies were initiated in 1979 by Derek Rayner, Prime Minister Margaret Thatcher's efficiency adviser. Most of the early scrutinies dealt with operational problems rather than policy questions and aimed at producing measurable savings through improved work methods. The typical study was confined to a single organisation and did not generate recommendations that could be applied across government departments. Each scrutiny team would undertake a short-term assignment, complete its review in about ninety days and go on to the next opportunity. In a 1986 report, *The Rayner Scrutinies Programmes 1979-93*, the National Audit Office found that the scrutinies "concentrated on the efficiency of aspects of a department's operations; relatively few scrutinies extended to the effectiveness of the expenditure in achieving policy objectives, and the larger and more difficult topics requiring substantial effort...". More than 350 scrutinies have been carried out over the past seventeen years under the guidance of the Efficiency Unit. (In fact, the Next Steps initiative was developed in one such scrutiny.) Nowadays, the process is highly structured and may be initiated to achieve value for money, to improve the quality of services, or to improve managerial performance. Some of the more recent scrutinies have had a broader, multi-departmental focus, but few have led to significant institutional – in contrast to procedural – change.

The limitations of the scrutinies led the Thatcher government to seek broader change through the Financial Management Initiative (FMI), which was launched in response to pressure from the Treasury and Civil Service Committee of Parliament. The government promoted FMI as a means of developing in each department an organisation and a system in which managers at all levels have:

- a clear view of their objectives and a means to assess and, wherever possible, measure outputs of performance in relation to those objectives;

– well-defined responsibility for making the best use of their resources, including a critical scrutiny of output and value for money; and

– the information (particularly about costs), the training, and access to expert advice they need to exercise their responsibilities effectively.

In line with its view that managers should take responsibility for performance, FMI did not prescribe a uniform approach for all departments. Progress depended on the willingness of top management to commit resources to FMI and to surrender some control over money and staff. A small financial management unit was set up in the Treasury, but it was neither large enough to devise new procedures for departments nor powerful enough to make significant inroads in the Treasury's expenditure and personnel systems. The unit's main role was to offer advice and monitor progress, not to dictate the terms under which departments delegated budgetary or other management responsibilities.

FMI did contribute to the upgrading of accounting systems and the measurement of performance and output. It also strengthened top management and policy development in some departments, and in its later stages spurred interest in delegated budgeting. The number of performance measures published in the Public Expenditure White Paper more than doubled, with even greater increases in output and effectiveness measures. But the enhancements in accounting and performance information brought little change in managerial behaviour. Four years after FMI was initiated, the National Audit Office reported that the new arrangements had not been in place long enough for their full effect, in terms of improved value for money, to become apparent. Progress was slowed by the Treasury's reluctance to delegate budgetary control before department managers conclusively demonstrated stronger competence in handling the enlarged responsibilities. The Treasury insisted that because of their responsibility for controlling the level of public expenditure, the central departments needed evidence of robust new systems before they could sensibly relax their existing control mechanisms. Foot-dragging also was practised by core departments, which persisted in controlling from headquarters, even when some controls were eased, as they were when departments were given increased flexibility in managing their running costs. Middle managers – those "budget holders" who were supposed to gain the most from the new flexibility – saw little benefit from FMI. Administrative practice was not much different than it had been before the reform was launched.

NEXT STEPS

FMI's disappointing progress set the stage for the Next Steps initiative, which was launched by the government in 1988. A 1988 report by the Efficiency Unit, *Improving Management in Government: The Next Steps*, concluded that far-reaching institutional changes would be necessary to uproot centralised, rule-bound management. Individual scrutinies had not sufficed, nor had modifications in procedure and improved information. After almost a decade of applying these remedies, the freedom of an individual manager to manage effectively and responsibly in the Civil Service was severely circumscribed. There were controls not only on resources and objectives, as there should be in any effective system, but also on the way in which resources can be managed. Recruitment, dismissal, choice of staff, promotion, pay, hours of work, the use of IT equipment, were all outside the control of most Civil Service managers at any level. The main decisions on rules and regulations were taken by the centre of the Civil Service. This tends to mean that they were structured to fit everything in general and nothing in particular. The rules were therefore seen primarily as a constraint rather than as a support; and in no sense as a pressure on managers to manage effectively.

Although it characterised recommended changes in the way departments operate as "fundamental and radical", the Next Steps report urged that reform "will need to be evolutionary". Reading between the lines of the report, one notices a reluctance to take on the departments directly, for doing so might have yielded the same meagre results that had resulted from previous initiatives. Instead, Next Steps moved by indirection. The core departments would not be reorganised, but the delivery of services would be hived off from them. What would remain, Next Steps anticipated, would be small departments responsible for policy guidance rather than big departments engaged in programme operations.

The report's key recommendation was that agencies "should be established to carry out the executive functions of government within a policy and resources framework set by a department." This pivotal recommendation raised more questions than it answered. Exactly what should be the relationship between the new agencies and the sponsor departments? Where should the line be drawn between agency and ministerial accountability for resources and results? To what extent should the civil service be reorganised along agency lines? These and other questions would be answered by practice, not by speculation as to how Next Steps might fundamentally change constitutional arrangements.

The launching of a Next Steps agency begins with the selection of a service as a candidate for agency status. The candidate agency then goes through "prior options" review – a series of questions concerning the appropriate role of government in financing or providing the service. First, does the particular activity need to be performed? If it is to be terminated, the review would end without an agency being established. Second, if the activity is to be carried out, should it be privatised or financed by public money? Third, if it is to be a public responsibility, can the work be contracted out? Finally, if the activity is to be provided and financed by government, should it be entrusted to an executive agency that has the independence and capacity to operate effectively?

The agencies vary greatly in size; the largest has 65 000 staff, the smallest only 30. To ensure a clear focus on priorities and objectives, Next Steps aims for each agency to have a single purpose, against which its performance can be measured and assessed. The prevailing belief is that giving an agency multiple purposes would muddle its objectives, lead to conflicting priorities, and complicate the task of monitoring performance. For example, the Benefits Agency, which is responsible for pensions, was initially assigned the task of obtaining child support from the legally responsible parents. It was thought, however, that this combination led to neglect of child support, which was, accordingly, split off into a separate agency. The singularity of purpose makes it possible to rely on a relatively small number of performance measures for each agency.

Each agency is headed by a chief executive selected in open competition unless the prime minister has authorised an internal candidate. Almost two-thirds of the chief executives appointed through 1994 were recruited via open competition; one-third have come from outside the civil service. The chief executive is personally responsible to the relevant minister for the performance of the agency, especially as regards agreed performance targets. A portion of the chief executive's pay normally is linked to achievement of the targets.

The launch of an agency and the appointment of its chief executive do not settle all issues concerning its operations. Every agency must work out its relationship with the parent department, not only in the framework document (discussed below) negotiated prior to launch, but also in ongoing operations. Each agency is independent in that it is responsible for its performance – with respect to both the resources used and the results achieved. But an agency also is legally dependent on the department which "owns" it and also may be the customer for its goods and services. Where the department is the only or the predominant customer, it may exercise close control by writing detailed contracts specifying each service to be provided. For example, the Ministry of Agriculture, Fisheries, and Food has a three-year contract for research to be conducted by the Central Veterinary Laboratory, one of the Next Steps agencies. In addition to this umbrella contract, more than two hundred annual contracts are negotiated for individual research projects, some for very small amounts of money. The full benefits of Next Steps status may not accrue to an agency that is so closely controlled by the parent department.

Even when departments give agencies room for manoeuvre, the relationship is often fuzzy. The chief executive normally serves as the accounting officer for the agency, but the permanent secretary serves as the departmental accounting officer. The chief executive answers to Parliament on matters concerning the agency's operation, but the minister is answerable to Parliament on all matters.

The government has repeatedly made it clear that Next Steps will involve no diminution in ministerial accountability to Parliament. It distinguishes between responsibility, which can be delegated, and accountability, which cannot. De facto, however, the establishment of executive agencies alters the roles of ministers and departments.

Next Steps requires that departments delegate but remain in charge. They must oversee but not intervene. They have to let go, while still being accountable for the performance of their agencies, especially when problems arise. Drawing the line between their proper scope of action and the need of agencies for managerial flexibility has not been easy. The first major assessment of Next Steps – the 1991 Fraser Report, *Making the Most of Next Steps* – concluded that departments were encroaching on agency prerogatives. It found "considerable frustration over the number of detailed and comparatively trivial management decisions which have to be referred back to sponsor departments or to the Treasury for approval". In response to the Fraser Report, the government urged that departments provide strategic advice and direction, not be involved in day-to-day operations. A report three years later, *Next Steps: Moving On*, found persistent problems in department-agency relations: "There exists a considerable cultural gap on both sides with Chief Executives often believing that Departments' management is a bureaucratic obstacle, and Departments viewing Agencies as little fortresses following their own aims regardless." It also noted "tensions between Departments and Agencies about the appropriate degree of flexibility. Agencies consider that they are almost separate from the Department and that they should have any flexibility required by their management. Departments, on the other hand, tend to examine only the cohesion and the uniformity of rules".

Despite the inevitable growing pains, the evidence points to significant progress in carving out agencies as management enclaves that are distinct from departments. Many agencies have reported dramatic gains in efficiency, far beyond the targets set for them. The new agencies exude a sense of freshness and excitement. Many have brought in new managers, not only at the top but also in the middle ranks where operating decisions are made. The creation of agencies has liberated them from encrusted controls and rules, perhaps not to the extent they would like, but far beyond what was the situation a few years ago. True, agencies complain about meddling departments, but the griping is stimulated by the freedom they have gained. They complain because they very much want to be in control of their own performance, and for the most part they are. For an agency newly empowered to act, any intervention by the department is apt to be seen as a trespass on its managerial discretion, but one should not mistake the complaints to mean that little has changed since the Next Steps were initiated.

Shortly after Next Steps was launched, the Treasury and Civil Service Committee of Parliament characterised this initiative as "the most ambitious attempt at Civil Service reform in the twentieth century." The committee, which often casts a sceptical eye at claimed progress in reforming public management, agreed that "the overall transformation in Government would not have been brought about without Next Steps." It expressed the belief "that Next Steps represent a significant improvement in the organisation of Government and that any future Government will want to maintain them in order to implement its objectives for the delivery of services to the public."

This favourable assessment has been confirmed in evaluations of individual agencies. When Next Steps was initiated, it was the announced policy that each agency be evaluated every three years. The current policy allows more flexibility and provides for an evaluation at least once every five years. The evaluations are conducted or commissioned by the sponsoring department. In evaluating the Employment Service, the parent department relied on sophisticated measures of outputs and outcomes, surveys of customer attitudes, and review of agency operations. It concluded that the establishment of the Employment Service "has created a firmly performance-driven organisation, clearly focused on achievement of its key objectives. This has led to continuing improvements in the quality of its services and the efficiency of their delivery." The Department of Social Security evaluated the Contributions Agency in the light of the performance targets set for it and found "substantial improvements in efficiency, effectiveness, and customer service." Not all assessments have been favourable, however. An evaluation of the Central Veterinary Laboratory by an outside consultant criticised the parent department for undue intervention in the agency's operation. Overall, however, there is impressive evidence that Next Steps has delivered on its promise of management improvement.

The improvement has been due largely to the infusion of new managerial talent and direction. The framework documents and performance targets have also provided impetus; thus far, however, the required medium-term corporate plans, annual business plans, and annual reports and accounts have made only modest contributions. The plans encourage the agency to prepare for the changes it expects to implement in the year ahead or over a three-year period and to organise work so as to accomplish the planned changes. But they do not spur much strategic thinking about the direction the agency should take. In view of the limited scope agencies have to redirect their objectives or activities, one should not expect the plans to have the same effect as they might have in private organisations or in departments. The annual reports and accounts provide data on the agency's financial condition and the extent to which it has met performance targets. The performance data in the reports are not subject to independent audit.

FRAMEWORK DOCUMENTS

At launch, each agency has a framework document (FD) that spells out the policy and resource framework within which it has to operate. The FD is negotiated by the agency and its parent department, with the Treasury looking over their shoulder to ensure that the government's interest in financial control and managerial devolution is satisfied. Although the Treasury guidelines insist that there can be no model FD – each should be tailored to the circumstances of the affected agency – they do have some common features. Each FD concisely sets forth the agency's role, its aims and objectives, the financial conditions under which it has to operate, the responsibilities of the chief executive, relations with the parent department and with the Treasury, accounting and audit arrangements, and delegations of financial or personnel responsibilities to the chief executive. The FD is not quite a full-fledged contract, but much more than an informal arrangement. It constitutes an understanding, hammered out in negotiations, as to what the agency will do, how it will be operated, and how the interested parties are to relate to one another.

Some participants in departments and agencies have suggested that the greatest value in the FD is in negotiating it. Drafting the FD requires that the "candidate" agency reflects on how it is to be transformed into an organisation that is accountable for performance. This is an empowering process that helps the agency develop the self-image necessary for it to operate effectively with a much greater degree of independence than was previously the case. It does not avert kinks in the relationship between the agency and its department, but it establishes ground rules and expectations for how the two entities are to interact. Although it sets forth various terms for the agency's operation, the FD appears to have less import once the agency has been launched. Department and agency officials do not refer to it every time they have a problem. When there is disagreement on their respective roles, the two sides must reach a fresh understanding; it does not suffice to say that the FD has already resolved the matter.

For agencies, the most salient portions of the FD may be the delegation of financial and personnel responsibilities. In some cases the language is general, but sometimes the delegation is quite specific as to what the agency may or may not do on its own accord. For example, the Veterinary Affairs Directorate's FD delegates financial authority to the chief executive in terms of threshold amounts below which he may act without obtaining prior approval of the department. The FD also lists more than a dozen services which may not be undertaken or contracted out without prior approval.

These delegations have been among the most controversial features of the FD. The basic principle is that an agency may exercise only the authority delegated to it. The Fraser report criticised departments for being niggardly in devolving financial and personnel responsibilities; it proposed "upside down" FDs that would delegate all authority not expressly withheld from agencies:

> *The objective should be to move to a position where agency Framework Documents establish that within the overall disciplines of the cash limits and targets set managers are free to make their own decisions on the management of staff and resources except for any specifically reserved area. The exclusion of any area from the chief executive's authority should be positively justified. The Order in Council should be amended at the earliest opportunity to permit such delegation.*

Initially, this recommended change in rules was not implemented because the Treasury and others objected that blanket delegation would be imprudent before an agency had demonstrated sufficient management capacity to warrant giving it full authority. But as Next Steps matured, agencies generally have exercised more independence in day-to-day operations than was the case in the first years of this initiative, and the principle has now been accepted that agencies may exercise any operational authority not withheld from them. This evolution has been propelled both by the agencies in gaining experience and by the departments in responding to pressures to downsize and adjust their roles to the new opportunities opened up by Next Steps.

The FD deals with relations between the agency and its department; it does not spell out relations between agency headquarters and the field or local offices that actually deliver services. The Treasury and Civil Service Committee of Parliament has argued that progress "does not simply require delegation *to* agencies; it requires delegation within agencies" (Fifth Report, 1993-94, 27-1 para. 156). Some larger entities have moved in this direction, most notably Inland Revenue (which is actually a department), which has delegated ongoing management responsibilities to its twenty-nine executive offices, and the Benefits Agency, which has issued a "Financial Management and Accountability" framework for its 159 district offices.

PERFORMANCE TARGETS

As has been noted, Next Steps agencies and chief executives are assessed in terms of annual performance targets set by ministers. Agencies also have internal targets that are elaborated in corporate and business plans; these typically are the basis for assessing results in the annual reports. In addition, the annual Next Steps Review reports on each agency's progress in meeting its key targets. Additional targets and milestones pertaining to the quality of service are issued pursuant to the Citizen's Charter. Finally, measurable progress in meeting targets is prominently featured in the periodic assessment of agencies. Although measuring and reporting on performance do not ensure improved performance, the sustained focus on results has sharpened agency attention to how well they are doing in meeting the targets.

Several characteristics of the targets distinguish them from previous efforts to measure performance. The targets concentrate on efficiency and outputs – matters within the direct control of the agency – rather than on outcomes and results. Just about every agency is targeted on financial performance (such as the percentage of costs recovered through user charges), efficiency (the percentage improvement over the previous year), and quality of service (such as the number of days taken to complete an action). Emphasis is placed on a small number of key targets by which the agency is judged rather than a large numbers of measures that represent the various things it does. These features are favoured because the principal function of the targets is to establish a basis for holding managers to account. For targets to serve as yardsticks of managerial performance, they must pertain to matters within the competence of the agency (hence, outputs rather than outcomes); they should be sufficiently few in number to permit a judgement as to whether the agency has performed as expected; and they must be measurable, so that the extent to which the targets have been achieved can be precisely stated.

These targets notify chief executives and other agency managers of what is expected of them by way of performance. The more precise and narrow the measure, the more powerfully it signals expected performance. The targets pressure agencies to raise their output, improve productivity, shorten response times, reduce customer complaints, recover a higher percentage of costs, and so on. Because the targets are so transparent, it is easy to determine whether an agency has lived up to expectations or fallen short. Occasionally, failure is so evident that the chief executive must be replaced. This occurred in the Child Support Agency established in 1991 to implement a new programme established that year by Parliament. Having a new agency start up a difficult programme from scratch was a prescription for failure. Performance data revealed that rather than clearing ordinary cases within 6-12 weeks, approximately 40 per cent took more than 100 days; and rather than arranging child support in 60 per cent of the eligible cases, the Agency arranged such payments in only about 30 per cent of the cases.

The pinpointed focus on measurable performance has come at some cost. The measures are not as challenging as has been claimed, nor as broad as might be desirable. Giving evidence before the Treasury and Civil Service Committee of Parliament in 1993, Sir Robin Butler, head of the Civil Service, argued: "Unless you set over ambitious targets, you don't get people to achieve more than they think they can achieve. All targets should be difficult for people to achieve." The problem with this formulation is that if targets were truly difficult, many would not be achieved. Rather than energising agencies to improve their performance, the targets might demoralise them, for no matter how much they tried, they still would fall short of the mark. Next Steps could not be deemed successful if agencies regularly failed to meet prescribed targets. Even if they improved, their performance would not be good enough. In fact, however, meeting the targets has been the norm for Next Steps agencies. In 1992-93, the government reported that agencies met 77 per cent of key performance targets; the next year, they met 80 per cent. The targets were set so that they could be reached, and most were. True, the achievements may require managerial effort and skill, but the task facing agencies is to reach targets that are within reach.

Targets are set by ministers, usually after negotiation with chief executives. They are not imposed unilaterally, nor are they set in disregard of the agency's judgement as to what can be reasonably expected. There is reason to believe that each year's targets are set with an eye to what was accomplished the previous year. At least in the largest agencies (those with more than 1 000 staff), some of the targets are unchanged from one year to the next, a few are lowered, and many are raised. When targets are raised, the changes usually are not dramatic. An agency that was targeted to increase efficiency by 4 per cent one year but actually achieved a much greater gain might aim for 4 per cent again the next year.

Output and efficiency targets narrow an agency's focus to matters of internal management, leading it to give less attention to broad policy questions. When the Financial Management Initiative (FMI) was undertaken, the government noted that the objective was not merely to improve the management of running costs but to stimulate improvements in programme effectiveness as well. The hope was that once managers were freed from detailed controls, they would have the opportunity and inclination to manage for results. The FMI did make some effort to measure progress in achieving policy objectives, but Next Steps seems to have retreated from that ambition. The logic of Next Steps calls for policy matters to be in the competence of departments and for agencies to be service providers. This division of responsibility leads to emphasising specific output measures of agency performance and broader policy measures for departments. Because departments have been slow in embracing a strategic role, progress in devising outcome measures has been quite limited.

The Treasury and Civil Service Committee of Parliament recommended that the targets be replaced by annual performance agreements between ministers and chief executives in 1994. The rationale offered by the committee had more to do with overall relations between departments and agencies than with the appraisal of performance. The Committee envisions negotiations over performance agreements as an opportunity to clarify relations between the agency and its department. These agreements would compensate for the failure of framework documents to offer sufficient guidance once an agency is operational. The negotiations would afford an opportunity to adjust department-agency roles in the light of recent experience and expectations, thereby encouraging a broader perspective than is typically taken in the target-setting process. But this broadening would run the risk of diffusing the sharp focus that makes performance targets so effective.

Recent government statements recognise the trade-off between pinpoint precision on the one hand and breadth on the other. The 1994 White Paper, *The Civil Service: Continuity and Change*, declares that "targets need to cover the breadth of an organisation's activities, to avoid resources being redirected toward areas where performance can be easily measured, and away from areas where measurement is more difficult." But the government remains committed to target-setting, in contrast to less pointed measures.

Consideration of performance measures would not be complete without mention of progress made under the Citizen's Charter in setting quality standards for services. The Charter requires that standards be set in absolute terms, so that users have information on the services they are entitled to expect. The development of service standards has been facilitated by media and public interest in this subject, the publication of their own charters by major agencies, and the issuance of Charter Mark awards for exceptional performance. While some critics have found fault with the promotional aspects of the Charter, the attention to service has undoubtedly brought visible improvements and greater sensitivity to customer needs and interests.

BEYOND NEXT STEPS

With the establishment of executive agencies expected to be completed by 1996, the government has taken additional steps to strengthen the managerial ethic in public organisations. The unfinished business includes market-testing and contracting out; reform of the civil service; restructuring central and core departments; and the introduction of resource (accrual) accounting and budgeting. The government has issued White Papers on the first three matters and a Green (discussion) Paper on the fourth. Although it would be premature to assess these initiatives, sufficient experience has accumulated to permit comment.

Marketisation

A 1991 White Paper, *Competing for Quality*, set forth the principle that, wherever practical, the provision of public services should be put out to competitive tender. Market testing is the procedure for determining whether it is feasible and efficient to contract out particular services. Departments are required to review their activities and identify those that may be suitable for a market test. Ideally, market testing should provide a "level playing field", with equal opportunity for public and private suppliers to compete, and without any presumption about the outcome. The winning bid would be the one that provides greater value for money, whether it comes from an in-house group or from a private source. In practice, however, the government sometimes has taken a strategic decision that it will not continue as a direct provider, thereby assuring that the winning bid will come from the private sector without any competing in-house bid. This practice has generated concern that market testing may undermine the managerial responsibility of agency executives. Rather than allowing the agency to determine how its services are to be provided, strategic contracting out predetermines that private bidders shall be the providers. In view of the government's interest in privatisation, there is concern that market testing is intended to shrink the size of the public sector.

This concern has been reinforced by periodic reports on the number of civil service posts eliminated by market testing. As of March 1994, for example, the government claimed a reduction of 14 500 positions, mostly due to increased contracting out. However, the government has moved to de-emphasise contraction in the civil service as an objective of market testing. "The Government does not believe", the 1994 Civil Service White Paper announces, "that staff numbers should be the primary focus of attention. Controlling staff numbers is not a particularly effective means of reducing costs and can perversely result in increased costs where more expensive substitutes for Civil Service staff are used simply because of the need to reduce numbers to predetermined levels." Furthermore, departments have been given greater leeway in selecting the means of enhancing value for money. Each department files an annual efficiency plan indicating the measures to be taken to operate within running costs limits. In addition to market testing, "departments will have more freedom than they do now to choose which levers to pull, and how hard to pull them."

Reform of the civil service

Managerial reform cannot proceed very far without an overhaul of the civil service. In the United Kingdom, as in other countries, complaints by managers are more likely to involve rigidities in the personnel system than financial restraints. But because the principle of uniformity and standardisation in the public service is so implanted in public administration, there has been considerable opposition to developing more flexible arrangements. Nevertheless, the establishment of Next Steps agencies has forced the question onto the reform agenda, for an agency cannot truly manage its operations if it lacks the freedom to employ and pay staff on the basis of performance. The authors of the 1988 Next Steps report foresaw the implications of establishing service delivery agencies for the civil service: "Ultimately some agencies could be in a position where they are no longer inside the Civil Service in the sense they are today. Any decision of this kind should be taken pragmatically – the test must always be adopting the structure which best fits the job to be done." When the government launched

Next Steps, Prime Minister Thatcher assured Parliament that the staff of the new agencies would continue to be civil servants. As Next Steps progressed and the implications for the civil service became more apparent, the government relied on an ambiguous formula – "unified but not uniform" – to describe the future civil service. Within the civil service, different arrangements would be encouraged to accommodate different circumstances.

"Unified but not uniform" has opened the door to different arrangements. In 1994 a number of the largest agencies took responsibility for their own pay bargaining. Moreover, agencies that operate as trading funds or have net (rather than gross) running cost control have flexibility in hiring staff if demand for their services rises. The 1994 Civil Service White Paper announced the government's intention to terminate national pay arrangements by giving responsibility for pay and grading of staff (except senior levels) to departments and agencies. Under the new regime, pay increases have to be financed by efficiencies and other savings, and expenditure on personnel has to be within agreed running costs. On paper, budget holders should now be fully responsible for personnel and financial resources. This "next step" will not be the last, for much depends on the extent to which pay arrangements are negotiated in departments or delegated to agencies. The White Paper asserted that "the Government is keen for each agency within a department to be responsible for its own pay and grading". Whether this materialises will depend on the extent to which the spirit of managerial reform reaches central and core departments.

Department reform

The slow pace of departmental reform has already been noted. In separating service-providing agencies from policy work, the government recognised that a frontal assault on Whitehall might have doomed Next Steps to the same disappointments as had beset previous efforts. Instead, it undermined the rationale for vast, central bureaucracies by stripping away some of the tasks they previously performed, especially those relating to personnel and financial management. Now that departments have less to do, or less justification for continuing to work as they once did, the time is ripe to align them to the new mode of devolved management. With pay delegation, that time has arrived.

The government has rejected one possible path to reform – extending Next Steps procedures to policy work in departments. While it accepts that Next Steps principles – such as the clear specification of objectives and targets, reporting on performance, and the delegation of management responsibility – should be applied to departments, the government does not envisage the formal establishment of agencies into areas of the Civil Service primarily concerned with policy. In these areas, the continued need for close ministerial involvement in the work and flexibility in organisation and management is not fully compatible with the clear delegation characteristic of agencies. Having rejected agency status, the government has promoted devolution by pressuring departments to downsize and concentrate on policy work. The expectation is that smaller departments will be less meddlesome departments; their reduced size will compel them to emphasise strategic management rather than day-to-day operations. In downsizing, layers of middle and senior managers involved in regulating the agencies are to be stripped away. What would remain after delayering would be lean organisations, clearly focused on questions of strategy and direction.

The shrinkage in departmental size and operations has been spurred by "Fundamental Expenditure Reviews" (FER). The FER is fundamental in the sense that it does not take existing work or arrangements for granted, but considers how the department would be organised and staffed if it were designed for a strategic role. The FER is undertaken by the affected department, which might make the examination less challenging than if an outside party did the work. But the aim is for the department to commit itself to the results of the review by conducting it. A departmental FER cannot be as readily disowned or ignored as one conducted by outsiders. Moreover, the FERs have been given teeth by reductions in the running costs allocated to departments. As they lose resources, departments have to ask what is worth doing and what might be divested or delegated. The answer differs among departments, but core departments no longer are as interventionist as they once were.

The role of central departments

The managerial discretion available to Next Steps agencies also depends on their relationship with the two central departments – the Treasury and the Office of Public Service. Despite the thrust toward devolution, all recognise that there must remain a role for the centre, but exactly what this role should be has occasioned some discussion. The 1990-91 report on Next Steps by the Treasury and Civil Service Committee of Parliament noted that "if power is to be devolved, the centre must have a clear idea of its role, and the necessary limits to the devolution of its powers. It is not enough to expect the role of agencies and their core departments to be clearly defined; such clarity must also be extended to the role of the Treasury..." In fact, the level of control exercised by the Treasury has been substantially reduced, particularly in the case of agencies.

The Next Steps: Moving On report concluded that agencies generally consider their relations with central departments to be better than with their own departments. There appears to be implicit collaboration in advancing the Next Steps initiatives between agencies and the central departments, a condition that is sometimes resented by departments which prefer, and sometimes demand, that contact with the agencies be done through them. If agencies have a problem, it is that the central departments appear to be unduly interventionist, producing numerous rules about how to manage and imposing initiatives on the agencies.

As a central department, the Treasury has participated in the FER process. In fact, it has taken the lead in self-examination and in implementing far-reaching organisational change on the basis of an FER completed in November 1994. Even before the FER, the Treasury was impelled by government-wide reforms to question its traditional role and operating procedures. It probably has been more strongly buffeted by the march of reform than any other governing institution. The Treasury entered the reform era as a controlling department. Although the doctrine of Treasury control (which had served as a model for other countries) had been relaxed by reforms in the 1960s (associated with introduction of the annual public expenditure survey), the Treasury remained heavily involved in examining the finances and, at times, personnel operations of departments and other governmental bodies. On the twin assumptions that spending departments could not be trusted to manage their own finances, and that failure to control the particulars of expenditure would weaken control of the totals, the Treasury exercised detailed surveillance of spending inputs.

The record suggests considerable doubt in government that a control-oriented Treasury would vigorously pursue management reform. Efficiency scrutinies, Next Steps, the Citizen's Charter, and market testing have all been assigned to separate units, not to the Treasury. When the FMI was launched, the Treasury established a separate unit that was faithful to the reform agenda and made some inroads in expenditure control, but had neither the mandate nor the resources to take on the role of the Treasury itself. With outsiders pushing for change, the Treasury sometimes found itself in the uneasy position of urging caution and insisting that existing controls not be divested until robust management systems were in place. For example, the Treasury counselled the government not to embrace the Fraser recommendation that each agency be presumed to have the financial and personnel delegations not expressly denied it. In this and other debates within government, it may not have been clearly seen that senior officials in the Treasury shared the new management ethic and that the Treasury has gone further in transforming itself than generally has been recognised. The Treasury has not been a naysayer standing in the way of progress. It has accepted the view that the control of spending totals is not well served by concentrating on the details, and it has taken initiative in developing the running cost arrangements that give budget holders greater freedom in administrative expenditure. It also has promoted delegated budgeting, broader application of performance measures, improvements in accounting and management information, and other initiatives, and it has issued a stream of guidances on new management practices. 129

The problem for the Treasury has not been satisfaction with the old ways but uncertainty about the pace of reform and about the role it might have in the new world of financial management. Looking back at the 1980s, one must acknowledge that it was a difficult period of adjustment for the Treasury. It knew what didn't work, but was unsure of what would, and how it would fit in. The doubts and the difficulties notwithstanding, the Treasury has made a remarkable transition. The "new" Treasury is an active promoter of management reform through instructions and manuals dealing with running cost control, annual reports and accounts, the establishment of Next Steps agencies, and much more. The Treasury is closely involved in setting up each agency; it participates in negotiating the framework document, recruiting the chief executive, financial and other delegations, reporting and accounting requirements, determining whether the agency should operate on a gross or net basis, selecting performance targets, and other management issues. The Treasury has become a guiding and prodding presence, and its staff has become increasingly at home in this role.

Inevitably, however, this transformation has had major implications for the size and structure of the Treasury. The main impact falls on the expenditure divisions, but all corners of the organisation have been affected. The implications were spelled out in the 1994 Fundamental Review that recommended a delayered Treasury with about 25 per cent fewer posts than previously. That Review fully supported "the more strategic approach now being developed to the control of department's running costs. We believe this should allow a further major streamlining of the resources the Treasury devotes to overseeing the management of other departments." The FER acknowledged that despite some devolution, the Treasury was still unduly involved in expenditure details. At the time the FER was conducted, the Treasury still exercised the following controls:

- it approved all spending on projects above a "delegated limit", even if the project was included in the department's capital budget as agreed in the public expenditure survey;

- it approved virements (transfers) within departmental budgets from one expenditure subhead to another, even when these did not affect total spending and were within cash or running cost limits;

- it approved routine special payments, losses and gifts that were not contentious and were within delegated limits;

- it commented on drafts of departmental reports and prepared reports on and approved departmental fees and charges.

The FER saw these requirements as "fairly inefficient tools for controlling departmental expenditure, for improving value-for-money, for seeking to influence the allocation of departmental resources, or simply obtaining information about how departments are spending their money." Taken together, it argued, "they do represent a perceptible irritant in the relationship between the Treasury and other departments."

In urging the divestiture of unproductive controls, the FER cautioned that the Treasury should "retain enough tools or levels to exercise their responsibilities effectively and efficiently – which in turn will require some departments to demonstrate a greater willingness to share management and financial information with the Treasury on a voluntary basis, than they have tended to show hitherto." The new relationship with departments should, FER suggested, be based on a "contract between the Treasury and each department setting out the rights, duties and obligations of each party in the relationship."

The transformation of the Treasury is far from complete and will entail short-term adjustments and long-term uncertainties. In the short run the Treasury must decide what to hold on to and what to let go; it must forge new working relationships with departments on a case-by-case basis. It must also re-examine relations with the other central departments responsible for public management, most notably the Office of Public Service and the Cabinet Office. Quite probably, the Treasury will go as far as it deems appropriate, and others will argue that it has not gone far enough. Adopting a new management style will not put an end to abrasions in relations with other departments, nor will it ensure that the boundaries are clearly marked. As long as there is a Treasury with power to act, there will be frictions, for the view from the centre will not always be the same as from other vantage posts.

The longer-term outlook is more problematic. The Treasury has carved out a niche in the launch process for agencies and in pushing management reform. For some years into the future, it can confidently expect to be productively occupied in issuing guidance and in promoting change. But at some point, agencies will be established and stabilised, departments will have gone through their own adjustments, and (as the logic of reform dictates) agencies and departments will have their own centres of management competence and innovation. It is not at all clear how the Treasury will fit in then – what levers it will have and what role it will play. One should not be surprised, therefore, if on the heels of the 1994 Fundamental Expenditure Review, the Treasury undertakes another review in the not-too-distant future.

Accrual accounting and budgeting

The final item on the current reform agenda is a shift from cash to accrual accounting. This shift was proposed in a 1994 Green Paper, *Better Accounting for the Taxpayer's Money: Resource Accounting and Budgeting in Government*. The basic recommendation was that government accounting should be based on commercial practices, "supplemented where appropriate to accommodate the particular requirements of central government." In making this threshold recommendation, the Green Paper had to dispose of several important questions. First, should control of cash be terminated or modified as accrual principles are introduced? Recognising the economic and political importance of cash receipts and expenditures, the government intends to meld the two approaches together. Public expenditure totals are to be expressed on an accruals basis, but Treasury and Parliament will still exercise "firm control over cash, reflecting the Government's responsibility to manage its own cash flow and borrowing. But cash control could be exercised at a less detailed level."

A second issue pertains to capital expenditure. Rather than having a separate capital budget, the accruals basis would allocate the cost of capital over the life of acquired assets. The operating budget would be charged (through depreciation or another charge) an amount representing the cost of capital. The third, and from the perspective of budget officials most important, issue is whether accruals should be applied only to financial statements and accounts or should be extended to budget presentations as well. The Green Paper concludes that the budget and the Public Expenditure Survey should be accounted for on the same basis as other financial statements. It notes that "the consistency of departments' internal budgeting systems with the overall system of budgetary allocation is a key objective of the proposed changes." Accrual budgeting would facilitate, it is argued, full costing of resources consumed and the development of unit cost measures of outputs, integration of capital and operating budget decisions, and (where appropriate) recovery of full costs through user charges. The government envisions a long transitional period before the new arrangements are fully operational.

Accrual accounting and budgeting would bring the reforms of the past dozen years full circle. Reform began with efforts to upgrade financial management; they were later broadened in recognition that financial reform could not take root in an inhospitable management environment. In Next Steps, therefore, the emphasis has been on management systems. Now the focus of reform is returning to financial practices, in recognition that managers cannot be fully productive if they lack information on the cost of resources. Accrual accounting and performance reporting should encourage advances in unit cost measurement. These measures have been sought for decades but have proven to be elusive. With the variety of cost measures available in the private sector infiltrating public management, it should be possible for managers to compare alternative delivery arrangements, assess the comparative efficiency of capital and operating expenditure, charge users, and improve the efficiency of services. By adopting commercial accounting practices, the government is signalling that it aims for public institutions to be managed as would well-run businesses, with one eye on costs and the other on outputs. Whether this ideal can be achieved without market incentives and pressures remains to be seen.

ASSESSING THE REFORMS

When it launched the Financial Management Initiative (FMI) in 1982, the Thatcher government characterised this reform as "a programme for the life of a Parliament and beyond". Although it foresaw that changing the rules and culture of public management would be a difficult and time-consuming task, the government did now know how long and arduous the modernisation process would be. More than a dozen years later, the work is far from done. In fact, the current government is busy with the latest flurry of innovations – reform of the civil service, accrual accounting and budgeting, efficiency plans, and fundamental expenditure reviews. The parade of reforms has induced "initiative fatigue" – weariness about the burgeoning demands on the shrinking ranks of government employees and weariness about what lies ahead. One manager interviewed for this study described himself as punch-drunk; another pleaded, "Can we just get our breath back, please." Some officials worry that the civil service will be splintered, with each agency (or department) running its own personnel system, and that the traditions of neutral competence will be weakened by the new managerial ethic. Some fear that the reforms are only transitional stages in a process that will culminate in the privatisation of important government functions. There is considerable uncertainty about relations between old departments and new agencies and where the line is to be drawn between managerial responsibility and ministerial accountability.

Yet there also is widespread agreement that the managerial revolution has accomplished much good. There has been genuine revitalisation of the public service, with an infusion of talented people, fresh ideas, and innovative work methods. Those interviewed share the view that entrusting responsibility to managers who provide the services makes more sense than trying to control just about everything from the centre and that the emphasis on performance has contributed more to programme effectiveness than did rule-driven control of inputs. They believe that the new ways have been sufficiently accepted and institutionalised so that the clock will not be turned back to the time, not very long ago, when the detailed provision of public services was managed in Whitehall. Most managers, in departments as well as in agencies, agree that basic reforms would survive a change in government, though some politically sensitive elements, such as market testing, might not. Most also agree that much remains to be done before the restructuring of government is completed.

Perhaps more than elsewhere, the British government can claim material success in changing the culture of public organisations. True, few agencies have been transformed into market- or performance-driven producers of public services; almost all remain public entities that operate under encumbrances and protections of government rules and authority. Nevertheless, measured against the centralised, control-oriented practices that once were the norm, progress has been impressive. The encumbrances and the rules are many fewer than they were a decade ago, concern about performance and exposure to efficiency-inducing incentives much greater, and the modernisation of work methods has been rapid. Most important, managers see themselves as managers empowered to do the work expected of them.

The reform agenda has been spurred by political stability and financial pressure. During more than fifteen consecutive years in government, the ruling Conservatives have been steadfast in their determination to reshape the public sector. Despite the relatively modest scope of the early reforms – the efficiency scrutinies started in 1979 and the Financial Management Initiative was launched three years later – the Thatcher-Major governments had an overarching vision of how public services should be managed. When some initiatives failed to produce the promised improvements, the government deepened the reforms and took bolder steps to make them work. Recent moves, especially Next Steps, have been more far-reaching than the earlier ones. The government has not deviated from its vision of a public sector in which managerial initiative is encouraged by the freedom to act and not quenched by *ex ante* controls, and it has had the staying power to accomplish much over a more than fifteen-year period.

The reforms have some unfinished business, or as yet unanswered questions. These pertain to the future character of the civil service, the role of the state, and accountability for governmental actions and policy outcomes. Civil service reform and the boundaries of the state are fundamental political questions whose resolution will likely depend on the results of future elections. But regardless of the political direction of future governments, new forms of accountability may have to be devised. Next Steps has not explicitly altered the constitutional principle of ministerial accountability to Parliament. The accepted principle is that ministers are responsible for policy, and chief executives are responsible for implementing the policy. In practice, the relationship is not so simple. In the tripartite relationship of minister, department permanent secretary and agency chief executive, the lines between political responsibility, strategic management, and operational control sometimes are blurred. It will take some time until the various responsibilities are sorted out.

MAIN SALES OUTLETS OF OECD PUBLICATIONS
PRINCIPAUX POINTS DE VENTE DES PUBLICATIONS DE L'OCDE

AUSTRALIA – AUSTRALIE
D.A. Information Services
648 Whitehorse Road, P.O.B 163
Mitcham, Victoria 3132   Tel. (03) 9210.7777
                                    Fax: (03) 9210.7788

AUSTRIA – AUTRICHE
Gerold & Co.
Graben 31
Wien I   Tel. (0222) 533.50.14
                                    Fax: (0222) 512.47.31.29

BELGIUM – BELGIQUE
Jean De Lannoy
Avenue du Roi, Koningslaan 202
B-1060 Bruxelles Tel. (02) 538.51.69/538.08.41
                                    Fax: (02) 538.08.41

CANADA
Renouf Publishing Company Ltd.
5369 Canotek Road
Unit 1
Ottawa, Ont. K1J 9J3   Tel. (613) 745.2665
                                    Fax: (613) 745.7660

Stores:
71 1/2 Sparks Street
Ottawa, Ont. K1P 5R1   Tel. (613) 238.8985
                                    Fax: (613) 238.6041

12 Adelaide Street West
Toronto, QN M5H 1L6   Tel. (416) 363.3171
                                    Fax: (416) 363.5963

Les Éditions La Liberté Inc.
3020 Chemin Sainte-Foy
Sainte-Foy, PQ G1X 3V6 Tel. (418) 658.3763
                                    Fax: (418) 658.3763

Federal Publications Inc.
165 University Avenue, Suite 701
Toronto, ON M5H 3B8   Tel. (416) 860.1611
                                    Fax: (416) 860.1608

Les Publications Fédérales
1185 Université
Montréal, QC H3B 3A7   Tel. (514) 954.1633
                                    Fax: (514) 954.1635

CHINA – CHINE
Book Dept., China National Publications
Import and Export Corporation (CNPIEC)
16 Gongti E. Road, Chaoyang District
Beijing 100020 Tel. (10) 6506-6688 Ext. 8402
                                    (10) 6506-3101

CHINESE TAIPEI – TAIPEI CHINOIS
Good Faith Worldwide Int'l. Co. Ltd.
9th Floor, No. 118, Sec. 2
Chung Hsiao E. Road
Taipei   Tel. (02) 391.7396/391.7397
                                    Fax: (02) 394.9176

**CZECH REPUBLIC –
RÉPUBLIQUE TCHÈQUE**
National Information Centre
NIS – prodejna
Konviktská 5
Praha 1 – 113 57   Tel. (02) 24.23.09.07
                                    Fax: (02) 24.22.94.33
E-mail: nkposp@dec.niz.cz
Internet: http://www.nis.cz

DENMARK – DANEMARK
Munksgaard Book and Subscription Service
35, Nørre Søgade, P.O. Box 2148
DK-1016 København K   Tel. (33) 12.85.70
                                    Fax: (33) 12.93.87

J. H. Schultz Information A/S,
Herstedvang 12,
DK – 2620 Albertslung   Tel. 43 63 23 00
                                    Fax: 43 63 19 69
Internet: s-info@inet.uni-c.dk

EGYPT – ÉGYPTE
The Middle East Observer
41 Sherif Street
Cairo   Tel. (2) 392.6919
                                    Fax: (2) 360.6804

FINLAND – FINLANDE
Akateeminen Kirjakauppa
Keskuskatu 1, P.O. Box 128
00100 Helsinki

Subscription Services/Agence d'abonnements :
P.O. Box 23
00100 Helsinki   Tel. (358) 9.121.4403
                                    Fax: (358) 9.121.4450

*FRANCE
OECD/OCDE
Mail Orders/Commandes par correspondance :
2, rue André-Pascal
75775 Paris Cedex 16 Tel. 33 (0)1.45.24.82.00
                                    Fax: 33 (0)1.49.10.42.76
                                    Telex: 640048 OCDE
Internet: Compte.PUBSINQ@oecd.org

Orders via Minitel, France only/
Commandes par Minitel, France
exclusivement : 36 15 OCDE

OECD Bookshop/Librairie de l'OCDE :
33, rue Octave-Feuillet
75016 Paris   Tel. 33 (0)1.45.24.81.81
                                    33 (0)1.45.24.81.67

Dawson
B.P. 40
91121 Palaiseau Cedex   Tel. 01.89.10.47.00
                                    Fax: 01.64.54.83.26

Documentation Française
29, quai Voltaire
75007 Paris   Tel. 01.40.15.70.00

Economica
49, rue Héricart
75015 Paris   Tel. 01.45.78.12.92
                                    Fax: 01.45.75.05.67

Gibert Jeune (Droit-Économie)
6, place Saint-Michel
75006 Paris   Tel. 01.43.25.91.19

Librairie du Commerce International
10, avenue d'Iéna
75016 Paris   Tel. 01.40.73.34.60

Librairie Dunod
Université Paris-Dauphine
Place du Maréchal-de-Lattre-de-Tassigny
75016 Paris   Tel. 01.44.05.40.13

Librairie Lavoisier
11, rue Lavoisier
75008 Paris   Tel. 01.42.65.39.95

Librairie des Sciences Politiques
30, rue Saint-Guillaume
75007 Paris   Tel. 01.45.48.36.02

P.U.F.
49, boulevard Saint-Michel
75005 Paris   Tel. 01.43.25.83.40

Librairie de l'Université
12a, rue Nazareth
13100 Aix-en-Provence   Tel. 04.42.26.18.08

Documentation Française
165, rue Garibaldi
69003 Lyon   Tel. 04.78.63.32.23

Librairie Decitre
29, place Bellecour
69002 Lyon   Tel. 04.72.40.54.54

Librairie Sauramps
Le Triangle
34967 Montpellier Cedex 2 Tel. 04.67.58.85.15
                                    Fax: 04.67.58.27.36

A la Sorbonne Actual
23, rue de l'Hôtel-des-Postes
06000 Nice   Tel. 04.93.13.77.75
                                    Fax: 04.93.80.75.69

GERMANY – ALLEMAGNE
OECD Bonn Centre
August-Bebel-Allee 6
D-53175 Bonn   Tel. (0228) 959.120
                                    Fax: (0228) 959.12.17

GREECE – GRÈCE
Librairie Kauffmann
Stadiou 28
10564 Athens   Tel. (01) 32.55.321
                                    Fax: (01) 32.30.320

HONG-KONG
Swindon Book Co. Ltd.
Astoria Bldg. 3F
34 Ashley Road, Tsimshatsui
Kowloon, Hong Kong   Tel. 2376.2062
                                    Fax: 2376.0685

HUNGARY – HONGRIE
Euro Info Service
Margitsziget, Európa Ház
1138 Budapest   Tel. (1) 111.60.61
                                    Fax: (1) 302.50.35
E-mail: euroinfo@mail.matav.hu
Internet: http://www.euroinfo.hu//index.html

ICELAND – ISLANDE
Mál og Menning
Laugavegi 18, Pósthólf 392
121 Reykjavik   Tel. (1) 552.4240
                                    Fax: (1) 562.3523

INDIA – INDE
Oxford Book and Stationery Co.
Scindia House
New Delhi 110001   Tel. (11) 331.5896/5308
                                    Fax: (11) 332.2639
E-mail: oxford.publ@axcess.net.in

17 Park Street
Calcutta 700016   Tel. 240832

INDONESIA – INDONÉSIE
Pdii-Lipi
P.O. Box 4298
Jakarta 12042   Tel. (21) 573.34.67
                                    Fax: (21) 573.34.67

IRELAND – IRLANDE
Government Supplies Agency
Publications Section
4/5 Harcourt Road
Dublin 2   Tel. 661.31.11
                                    Fax: 475.27.60

ISRAEL – ISRAËL
Praedicta
5 Shatner Street
P.O. Box 34030
Jerusalem 91430   Tel. (2) 652.84.90/1/2
                                    Fax: (2) 652.84.93

R.O.Y. International
P.O. Box 13056
Tel Aviv 61130   Tel. (3) 546 1423
                                    Fax: (3) 546 1442
E-mail: royil@netvision.net.il

Palestinian Authority/Middle East:
INDEX Information Services
P.O.B. 19502
Jerusalem   Tel. (2) 627.16.34
                                    Fax: (2) 627.12.19

ITALY – ITALIE
Libreria Commissionaria Sansoni
Via Duca di Calabria, 1/1
50125 Firenze   Tel. (055) 64.54.15
                                    Fax: (055) 64.12.57
E-mail: licosa@ftbcc.it

Via Bartolini 29
20155 Milano   Tel. (02) 36.50.83

Editrice e Libreria Herder
Piazza Montecitorio 120
00186 Roma   Tel. 679.46.28
                                    Fax: 678.47.51

Libreria Hoepli
Via Hoepli 5
20121 Milano   Tel. (02) 86.54.46
                        Fax: (02) 805.28.86

Libreria Scientifica
Dott. Lucio de Biasio 'Aeiou'
Via Coronelli, 6
20146 Milano   Tel. (02) 48.95.45.52
                        Fax: (02) 48.95.45.48

JAPAN – JAPON
OECD Tokyo Centre
Landic Akasaka Building
2-3-4 Akasaka, Minato-ku
Tokyo 107   Tel. (81.3) 3586.2016
                        Fax: (81.3) 3584.7929

KOREA – CORÉE
Kyobo Book Centre Co. Ltd.
P.O. Box 1658, Kwang Hwa Moon
Seoul   Tel. 730.78.91
                        Fax: 735.00.30

MALAYSIA – MALAISIE
University of Malaya Bookshop
University of Malaya
P.O. Box 1127, Jalan Pantai Baru
59700 Kuala Lumpur
Malaysia   Tel. 756.5000/756.5425
                        Fax: 756.3246

MEXICO – MEXIQUE
OECD Mexico Centre
Edificio INFOTEC
Av. San Fernando no. 37
Col. Toriello Guerra
Tlalpan C.P. 14050
Mexico D.F.   Tel. (525) 528.10.38
                        Fax: (525) 606.13.07
E-mail: ocde@rtn.net.mx

NETHERLANDS – PAYS-BAS
SDU Uitgeverij Plantijnstraat
Externe Fondsen
Postbus 20014
2500 EA's-Gravenhage   Tel. (070) 37.89.880
Voor bestellingen: Fax: (070) 34.75.778

Subscription Agency/Agence d'abonnements :
SWETS & ZEITLINGER BV
Heereweg 347B
P.O. Box 830
2160 SZ Lisse   Tel. 252.435.111
                        Fax: 252.415.888

**NEW ZEALAND –
NOUVELLE-ZÉLANDE**
GPLegislation Services
P.O. Box 12418
Thorndon, Wellington   Tel. (04) 496.5655
                        Fax: (04) 496.5698

NORWAY – NORVÈGE
NIC INFO A/S
Ostensjoveien 18
P.O. Box 6512 Etterstad
0606 Oslo   Tel. (22) 97.45.00
                        Fax: (22) 97.45.45

PAKISTAN
Mirza Book Agency
65 Shahrah Quaid-E-Azam
Lahore 54000   Tel. (42) 735.36.01
                        Fax: (42) 576.37.14

PHILIPPINE – PHILIPPINES
International Booksource Center Inc.
Rm 179/920 Cityland 10 Condo Tower 2
HV dela Costa Ext cor Valero St.
Makati Metro Manila   Tel. (632) 817 9676
                        Fax: (632) 817 1741

POLAND – POLOGNE
Ars Polona
00-950 Warszawa
Krakowskie Prezdmiescie 7 Tel. (22) 264760
                        Fax: (22) 265334

PORTUGAL
Livraria Portugal
Rua do Carmo 70-74
Apart. 2681
1200 Lisboa   Tel. (01) 347.49.82/5
                        Fax: (01) 347.02.64

SINGAPORE – SINGAPOUR
Ashgate Publishing
Asia Pacific Pte. Ltd
Golden Wheel Building, 04-03
41, Kallang Pudding Road
Singapore 349316   Tel. 741.5166
                        Fax: 742.9356

SPAIN – ESPAGNE
Mundi-Prensa Libros S.A.
Castelló 37, Apartado 1223
Madrid 28001   Tel. (91) 431.33.99
                        Fax: (91) 575.39.98
E-mail: mundiprensa@tsai.es
Internet: http://www.mundiprensa.es

Mundi-Prensa Barcelona
Consell de Cent No. 391
08009 – Barcelona   Tel. (93) 488.34.92
                        Fax: (93) 487.76.59

Libreria de la Generalitat
Palau Moja
Rambla dels Estudis, 118
08002 – Barcelona
            (Suscripciones) Tel. (93) 318.80.12
            (Publicaciones) Tel. (93) 302.67.23
                        Fax: (93) 412.18.54

SRI LANKA
Centre for Policy Research
c/o Colombo Agencies Ltd.
No. 300-304, Galle Road
Colombo 3   Tel. (1) 574240, 573551-2
                Fax: (1) 575394, 510711

SWEDEN – SUÈDE
CE Fritzes AB
S–106 47 Stockholm   Tel. (08) 690.90.90
                        Fax: (08) 20.50.21

For electronic publications only/
Publications électroniques seulement
STATISTICS SWEDEN
Informationsservice
S-115 81 Stockholm   Tel. 8 783 5066
                        Fax: 8 783 4045

Subscription Agency/Agence d'abonnements :
Wennergren-Williams Info AB
P.O. Box 1305
171 25 Solna   Tel. (08) 705.97.50
                        Fax: (08) 27.00.71

Liber distribution
Internatinal organizations
Fagerstagatan 21
S-163 52 Spanga

SWITZERLAND – SUISSE
Maditec S.A. (Books and Periodicals/Livres
et périodiques)
Chemin des Palettes 4
Case postale 266
1020 Renens VD 1   Tel. (021) 635.08.65
                        Fax: (021) 635.07.80

Librairie Payot S.A.
4, place Pépinet
CP 3212
1002 Lausanne   Tel. (021) 320.25.11
                        Fax: (021) 320.25.14

Librairie Unilivres
6, rue de Candolle
1205 Genève   Tel. (022) 320.26.23
                        Fax: (022) 329.73.18

Subscription Agency/Agence d'abonnements :
Dynapresse Marketing S.A.
38, avenue Vibert
1227 Carouge   Tel. (022) 308.08.70
                        Fax: (022) 308.07.99

See also – Voir aussi :
OECD Bonn Centre
August-Bebel-Allee 6
D-53175 Bonn (Germany) Tel. (0228) 959.120
                        Fax: (0228) 959.12.17

THAILAND – THAÏLANDE
Suksit Siam Co. Ltd.
113, 115 Fuang Nakhon Rd.
Opp. Wat Rajbopith
Bangkok 10200   Tel. (662) 225.9531/2
                        Fax: (662) 222.5188

**TRINIDAD & TOBAGO, CARIBBEAN
TRINITÉ-ET-TOBAGO, CARAÏBES**
Systematics Studies Limited
9 Watts Street
Curepe
Trinidad & Tobago, W.I. Tel. (1809) 645.3475
                        Fax: (1809) 662.5654
E-mail: tobe@trinidad.net

TUNISIA – TUNISIE
Grande Librairie Spécialisée
Fendri Ali
Avenue Haffouz Imm El-Intilaka
Bloc B 1 Sfax 3000   Tel. (216-4) 296 855
                        Fax: (216-4) 298.270

TURKEY – TURQUIE
Kültür Yayinlari Is-Türk Ltd.
Atatürk Bulvari No. 191/Kat 13
06684 Kavaklidere/Ankara
                Tel. (312) 428.11.40 Ext. 2458
                Fax : (312) 417.24.90

Dolmabahce Cad. No. 29
Besiktas/Istanbul   Tel. (212) 260 7188

UNITED KINGDOM – ROYAUME-UNI
The Stationery Office Ltd.
Postal orders only:
P.O. Box 276, London SW8 5DT
Gen. enquiries   Tel. (171) 873 0011
                        Fax: (171) 873 8463

The Stationery Office Ltd.
Postal orders only:
49 High Holborn, London WC1V 6HB
Branches at: Belfast, Birmingham, Bristol,
Edinburgh, Manchester

UNITED STATES – ÉTATS-UNIS
OECD Washington Center
2001 L Street N.W., Suite 650
Washington, D.C. 20036-4922
                        Tel. (202) 785.6323
                        Fax: (202) 785.0350
Internet: washcont@oecd.org

Subscriptions to OECD periodicals may also
be placed through main subscription agencies.

Les abonnements aux publications périodiques
de l'OCDE peuvent être souscrits auprès des
principales agences d'abonnement.

Orders and inquiries from countries where Dis-
tributors have not yet been appointed should be
sent to: OECD Publications, 2, rue André-Pascal, 75775 Paris Cedex 16, France.

Les commandes provenant de pays où l'OCDE
n'a pas encore désigné de distributeur peuvent
être adressées aux Éditions de l'OCDE, 2, rue
André-Pascal, 75775 Paris Cedex 16, France.

12-1996

OECD PUBLICATIONS, 2, rue André-Pascal, 75775 PARIS CEDEX 16
PRINTED IN FRANCE
(42 97 09 1 P) ISBN 92-64-15678-X – No. 49799 1997